LEGENDARY SHOW JUMPERS

AMAZING STORIES

LEGENDARY SHOW JUMPERS

The Incredible Stories of Great Canadian Horses

ANIMAL/SPORT

by Debbie Gamble-Arsenault

PUBLISHED BY ALTITUDE PUBLISHING CANADA LTD.
1500 Railway Avenue, Canmore, Alberta T1W 1P6
www.altitudepublishing.com
1-800-957-6888

Extreme care has been taken to ensure that all information presented in
this book is accurate and up to date. Neither the author nor the
publisher can be held responsible for any errors.

Publisher	Stephen Hutchings
Associate Publisher	Kara Turner
Series Editor	Jill Foran
Editors	Audrey McClellan, Jill Foran

We acknowledge the financial support of the Government
of Canada through the Book Publishing Industry Development
Program (BPIDP) for our publishing activities.

Altitude GreenTree Program
Altitude Publishing will plant twice as many trees as were used
in the manufacturing of this product.

National Library of Canada Cataloguing in Publication Data

CIP data is available on request from the publisher

ISBN: 1-55153-980-2

An application for the trademark for Amazing Stories™
has been made and the registered trademark is pending.

Printed and bound in Canada by Friesens
2 4 6 8 9 7 5 3 1

The cover photograph shows Ian Millar riding Big Ben.
(Photo by Cealy Tetley)

Dedication

For my grandmother, "Grammy Robin" (Hilda King Robinson), who read to me when I was little and always encouraged my "artistic" side.

For my parents, Jeanne and Aubrey Gamble, who raised us with love and, realizing the importance of reading, always gave us books.

For my husband, Tim Arsenault, who by showing the courage to go back to school, inspired *me* to try something new.

For my family, who've always accepted my writing, this crazy thing that I do.

And most of all, for Julie V. Watson, who befriended me, mentored me, encouraged me, and most of all, believed in me. I am forever grateful. Thank you, "Jewels" ... you are a pearl without price.

Author's Note

Throughout this book I make reference to horses being so many "hands high," commonly written as "hh."

We measure the height of horses from the ground to the top of the withers — where the neck joins the shoulders — and traditionally it is done in "hands." One hand equals 4 inches or 10 centimetres; therefore, a horse said to be 16 hh would be 160 centimetres at the withers.

In addition, height is read in hands and inches, so a horse noted as 16.3 hh would be 16 hands, plus 3 inches tall, or 167.5 centimetres tall.

Contents

Prologue

As a child, you always dreamed of learning to ride and becoming a famous show jumper someday, but circumstances put that dream on the back burner. Now, however, the time is right.

You've been taking lessons from a competent and caring riding coach; you've made encouraging progress in your flat work, trotted over cavalletti poles, and even popped over some low jumps. Today's the big day: your first lesson over multiple jumps. Today you learn how to fly.

"Okay, remember what we practised," says Judy, your coach, as you tack up Spook, a flashy yet elegant bay Appaloosa gelding with a white-blanketed rump that looks like someone threw a white sheet over his hind end, then splashed it with large spots of dark brown paint.

"Begin at the walk, out along the rail. Cue him to a trot and then, in the corner, ease him into a canter, turn in, and go down the line.

"There are only three small jumps, set at one foot six inches, two feet, and two foot three," she continues.

"They're easy. Don't rush them, and don't be afraid. You can do it. I have confidence in you!"

With your heart in your throat, you do as Judy has directed, muttering all her instructions from previous lessons under your breath. Heels down, knees in, elbows close to your sides, leg aid on, reins, position ... There's so much to remember.

So far, so good. Spook has picked up a slow, controlled canter perfectly, and you turn him in towards the line of jumps. But from here they look a lot higher — more like 10 feet high than two feet. Your heart begins to pound harder, you stiffen up, and your fingers take a stranglehold on the reins as the jumps loom closer, ever closer ...

With his head weaving from one side to the other due to your uncertain guidance, Spook canters more and more slowly as he approaches the first element. At the designated take-off point, he stops, steps delicately over the first jump, stops again, and turns his head back to look at you quizzically, as if to say, "Now what?"

Embarrassed, and blushing madly, you glance shamefacedly at Judy ... and you both burst into laughter. "You were giving him mixed signals," she giggles. "Your legs were saying, 'Go on, jump,' but your mind and hands were saying, 'Stop! Stop!' With your instructions in such a muddle, Spook simply went on his own best judgment.

Prologue

"Okay, take him around and try again," Judy urges. "This time, give him a bit longer rein — don't choke him off. Keep the same amount of leg on and you'll do fine. Find the rhythm of the jumps," she points out. "Canter, canter, jump. Two strides, jump. Three strides, jump. That's all there is to it. Off you go!"

"I hope not," you mutter as you rein Spook around and trot off for the second try. Fiercely determined to get it right this time, you follow Judy's instructions and approach the first jump again, cajoling yourself, "Okay, Self, here we go. Canter, canter …" At exactly the right moment you rise into the two-point position, move your hands up Spook's neck to give him enough rein, and suddenly you feel lighter than air.

The wind whistles past your ears. Spook's muscles bunch and flex beneath you. What power! Up and over; touch down lightly; stride, stride; aloft over the second element; stride, stride, stride; a bigger effort at jump number three, and then, all too soon, the end.

You slow your mount to a walk, beaming with pleasure as Judy applauds. You've done it. You've successfully piloted a high-flying horse over your first jump combination. What was there to be scared about? Suddenly, you realize you're hooked …

Chapter 1
In the Beginning

Never mind that the two horses and their riders were tired, or that some dangerous ground lay between them and the ultimate goal. The honour of both men, and their belief and pride in their mounts, was at stake.

The competition started innocently enough. At the end of a long and arduous day of foxhunting, O'Callaghan and Blake had been making their way homeward. A taste of the stirrup-cup — the traditional drink offered to riders at the start of a day of hunting — had been augmented by nips from their pocket flasks throughout the day as they toasted each good draw of scent, the successful hunt, and even each other. (Truth be told, the soothing libation, the day's exertion, and the fresh air had made both the men quite tipsy, relaxed, and happy.)

O'Callaghan was well pleased with the results of the splendiferous day. His fast, brave, big-jumping Irish Mist had followed gamely right behind the Master of the Hunt all day, leaping whatever obstacle stood in his way without any refusal or second look. O'Callaghan had been close enough to the action at the end of the hunt to see the hounds finish off the fox.

Usually a nose-to-the-grindstone sort of person, O'Callaghan felt not one iota of regret at leaving his son to oversee the running of the farm. This day had given him some never-to-be-forgotten memories.

Blake was equally jubilant. He had prevented the fox from going to ground by blocking Reynard's escape route long enough for the hounds to catch him up, and for that, Blake had received the brush and mask.

The fact of the matter was that Blake and his horse, Donegal, had become separated from the field, as well as slightly lost, and had stopped to take a breather. When the fox circled back around to lose the hounds, it ended up in the same spot where the horse and rider were resting. That he had been in just the right place at just the right time more by good luck than good management was forgotten now as Blake congratulated himself on his prowess in the hunting field. For that shining moment, he had risen from being a simple farmer to become a "hard man to hounds."

As horsemen do at the end of a satisfying day, the two began to regale each other with the exploits and virtues of their respective mounts. They were ambling peaceably past Buttervent Church when O'Callaghan bragged, "And did ye see that larripin' big lep my fine Mist took at Murphy's stone wall? Sure and no other horse in the whole of Ireland could have done it better. 'Tis none so brave and fine as he." O'Callaghan leaned over and gave his horse a prideful pat on the side of the neck.

"Away with ye, O'Callaghan," Blake chided his friend. "'Twas me and my own Donegal was right on yer tail at that wall, and pullin' to pass ye, he was. 'Twere only by the grace o' God — and me own skilful ridin', mind! — that we didn't run over the pair o' ye." Donegal snorted explosively, as if to punctuate Blake's boastful statement. (One can do few worse things to an Irishman than insult his horse; both men would have done well to remember that.)

O'Callaghan pulled Mist to a halt and stared at his compatriot in amazement and outrage. "The day *yer* rack o' bones can pass *my* good-as-gold Mist, boyo, will be the day I don a petticoat 'n' curls, 'n' become a tavern wench," he jeered.

"Rack o' bones?" Blake spluttered. "Me beautiful Donnie-boy can outrun and outjump that swaybacked, bog-spavined pony of yours with a league's head start, any day, any time."

"Pony? Pony!" O'Callaghan howled, incensed, shaking his fist at the other man. Irish Mist was a robust, well-muscled blood horse, by the famous sire Armagh Warrior, a grandson of the Godolphin Arabian, out of an equally finely bred mare, and he was a strapping 16 hands into the bargain. In O'Callaghan's eyes, calling his pride and joy a *pony* was the ultimate affront.

The gauntlet had been thrown down; the matter must be resolved. Casting a look around the countryside, O'Callaghan's eyes lit on the steeple of St. Leger Church, far away across the valley. Suddenly, inspiration hit.

"All right, then," he challenged. "If yer Donegal is so bloody good, he'll not be having a problem beating me and Mist to yon church. First one there and touches the front door is the winner and has the better horse. Are ye man enough t'accept the contest?"

Blake paled and tugged at his shirt collar. St. Leger was nearly 10 miles away — and between it and Buttervent Church lay some of the hilliest, rockiest, most densely wooded land in the entire county. But he had run off at the mouth, bragging about Donegal, and now he had to pay the piper. Manfully, he faced O'Callaghan squarely and stuck out his hand.

"All right, then, shake on it," he said. And O'Callaghan did. They tightened loosened girths, gathered loose reins, and lined up side by side. The horses, which until now had been plodding along like placid old stable hacks for hire, sensed their masters' excitement and began dancing and jigging in anticipation.

"On my word, go," O'Callaghan instructed, then immediately shouted "Go!" With a great lunge, they were off.

Because O'Callaghan was the one who gave the signal to start, he got the jump on Blake and was a horse's length ahead as they cleared the first fence and thundered over the winter-dry grass of Jack Killorn's 10-acre field. Up, over, and out, galloping onward, ever onward, through meadow and field, over hill and dale. The wild grasses at the edge of the road bent at the rush of their passing, as though before the onslaught of a powerful wind.

Helter-skelter, they crossed the high road and took a huge leap over a hawthorn hedge into a rock-strewn pasture, horseshoes striking sparks off stone as they clattered forward, dodging slumbering sheep and startled lambs.

In the Beginning

Through Wharraton Wood, where a solid oak branch nearly swept Blake from the saddle when Donegal ducked under it rather than go around the tree. A covey of quail, flushed from their hiding place by the riders' yells to their horses, exploded into the air practically under Irish Mist's nose, which caused the horse a moment of panicked surprise; however, he recovered quickly and galloped strongly forward.

On and on they went, Irish Mist sometimes in front, Donegal stealing the lead at other times, but always their riders urging them, beseeching them to greater speed. The men kept their eyes glued to the steeple of St. Leger as the distance between them and their goal lessened.

Stirrup to stirrup, they charged through a gate and across the expanse of a hayfield. They cleared the drystone wall that marked the field's boundaries, and as they did — in mid-jump in fact — O'Callaghan was horrified to discover that what lay beyond the wall was a sprightly babbling brook, glistening in the weak winter sun and burbling joyously as it tumbled over its rocky bed. Its watery laughter sounded like hoots of derision and doom in O'Callaghan's ears. If Irish Mist had a fault, it was that he hated getting his feet wet and would do anything to avoid it. In that split second between discovery and disaster, O'Callaghan braced himself for the inevitable.

Irish Mist saw the brook, performed the equine equivalent of a double-take, and then twisted himself in midair, loath to land in the brook. With superlative effort — and a large dose of luck — he cleared the brook but stumbled on landing, nearly falling to his knees. O'Callaghan was yanked out of the saddle and almost over Mist's ears. Donegal surged ahead, and Blake yelled, "Be seein' ya at church, boyo!" as the pair fled away towards the ultimate goal.

After a brief but taxing struggle, O'Callaghan managed to drag himself back into the saddle, while his gallant horse regained his feet and resumed the chase. Blake and Donegal were many lengths ahead, but Irish Mist was nothing if not game, and he resumed the powerful rhythm of his gallop as he put his all into catching up to the disappearing Donegal. "Come on, me lovely, come on," O'Callaghan crooned and cajoled, flattening himself along Mist's neck as the wind rushed past. "Ye can do it, I know ye can."

By now, exhausted muscles were protesting, overtaxed lungs were heaving, and every stride was an effort. But the hot blood of competitive horses coursed through Irish Mist's veins, and he was as arrogant as he was fast and beautiful. Coming in second was unthinkable; getting his nose in front was all. He pinned back his ears, stretched out his neck, stuck out his muzzle, levelled out even more with his ground-eating stride, and refused to give in.

Blake looked back in dismay as O'Callaghan and Mist bore down on him and Donegal. Their opponents were only four horse-lengths behind, then three, moving ever closer with vengeful purpose, like one of the four horsemen of the Apocalypse. The power and grace of Mist's stride was a fearful thing to see.

Frantically, Blake gave his horse a sharp tap with the whip, and Donegal gallantly responded with yet another burst of speed. But Irish Mist would not be denied.

With three great bounds, he caught up to Donegal and then stubbornly won back the lead, inch by painful inch. He was a neck ahead of Donegal as they cleared the boundary fence into the churchyard, scattering gaping villagers in all directions as a fox scatters pullets in a henhouse. With one final spectacular leap, Irish Mist skidded to a halt at the front of the church as O'Callaghan leaned far out of the saddle to give the door a triumphant slap. "We win!" he gasped, exultant, as Donegal slid to a stop practically on Mist's heels.

Both horses stood, spraddle-legged, heads low, ears at half mast, and sides heaving. Equally spent, the two men oozed from their saddles and sat on the church doorstep to regain their breath and composure. When they could finally speak, Blake ruefully offered his hand to O'Callaghan and said, "I concede, my friend. Your horse *is* better than mine."

"Thank ye fer sayin' that, friend. Mist *did* do well, didn't he?" said O'Callaghan, basking in the glory of victory and the admiration of his friend. "But ye gave it a fine try, Blake. My hat's off to ye and Donegal both. Between us, we've the two best horses in the whole of Ireland.

"Now, let's be gettin' these laddies home t'some bran mash and a warm stable," he said with a soft laugh as he struggled, groaning, to his feet and prepared to remount. "They both deserve t'be treated like royalty ..."

High-Flying Facts
The previous account is a work of fiction from the imagination of the author. Only the names of the men and the churches are real. The story does reflect, however, the truth about the origins of the steeplechase. Riders and their hunting horses had to learn to jump all manner of different types of fences when British farmland began to be enclosed in the 18th century. Attention to bloodlines and breeding resulted in faster horses, which naturally led to disputes over the speed and ability of those horses.

These disputes were often settled by running

match races across the countryside. Since churches were very visible landmarks, they were often used as start and finish points for these impromptu races, which were dubbed steeplechases. In 1752, a Mr. Blake and a Mr. O'Callaghan raced each other from Buttervent Church to St. Leger Church in Ireland.

In 1810, Bedlam, England was the site of the first race ever recorded over a prepared steeplechase course with fences made specifically for that purpose. The granddaddy of all steeplechases, the Grand National Steeplechase, was established at Liverpool, England in 1837.

The wild thrills of a steeplechase race were obviously addictive, because the sport was eventually brought to North America in the early 19th century.

The Mists of Time
No one knows precisely when humans started riding horses over high jumps, but we do know that an attraction for the thrill of flying through the air with a good horse under you surfaced early in our equine history.

Foxhunting has been around for thousands of years. Alexander the Great (356–323 B.C.) took time out from his many war campaigns to enjoy foxhunting in parts of Asia, and Persian history records show foxhunting on horseback was taking place by 4 B.C. Foxhunting with hounds is recorded to have happened in both Thrace (now Istanbul, Turkey) and Italy by about A.D. 80. British officers, enthusiastic about their horses and hunting, took the sport with them wherever they went. The colonization of foreign countries under the British crown required that the British army be in residence. Consequently, British officers were largely responsible for the spread of foxhunting traditions to Africa, New Zealand, Australia, and India, where, instead of foxes, they hunted the fox's cousin, the jackal.

The arrival in Maryland of Robert Brooke, his family, and his hounds on June 30, 1650, is the earliest report of hounds being imported to North America. An avid hunter from the age of 16, George Washington owned both an excellent pack of hounds and a stable of finely bred horses to enable him to enjoy his passion. Thomas Jefferson was also an ardent foxhunting aficionado.

Embraced by nearly every part of America, the sport became most popular in the mid-south, which had maintained many of the aristocratic English traditions and still had large, unfenced land masses ideally suited for the chase.

The Montreal Hunt was the first foxhound club in Canada; it was established in 1826. The first steeplechase organized in North America was also held in the area of Montreal. The Montreal Steeplechase course of 1840 was three miles long, featuring numerous brooks and 20 obstacles.

Why Do They Do It?

Who could deny the attraction of an exhilarating day on horseback, a staggering variety and number of fences taken at speed, and the sheer joy of spending time with your favourite mount, in the company of others who enjoy riding as much as you do?

Foxhunting is horses, hounds, and humans in blissful partnership, revelling in the exhilaration of searching out one of the most cunning creatures in the animal kingdom, while enjoying Nature's beauty. Riding the horse allows man to keep pace with the hounds as they seek their quarry. The rider is party to the sights, smells, and sounds of the hunt: the streaking rust-red blur of the fox, pursued by the black, white, and tan-coloured pack; the rich, earthy smell of the ground, the trees, and the fields; and the deep, full-bodied baying of the hounds, accompanied by the thunder of many hooves and the brassy sound of the huntsman's horn as it echoes over hill and dale. No two chases are the same, and every new hunt is a unique experience.

An old poem called "The Fox and the Owl," by that great writer Anonymous, also illustrates the romance of chasing a wily fox high, wide, and handsome over the picturesque countryside. This poem was handed down to me by my maternal grandfather, Nelson H. Robinson (1902–1995), who learned it at *his* grandmother's knee.

> *But I'll tell Jack, with his hounds and his horn ...*
> *And the bow-wow dogs, and the toot-toot horn,*
> *and the galloping horse, and Jack*
> *Will race you and trace you wherever they chase*
> *you, and thunder along your track.*
>
> *So the next morning, out came Jack, with his*
> *spurs on his heels, and his whip to crack,*
> *And saddled his horse, and called for his pack,*
> *and started off on the fox's track.*
> *Away they went with the clattering sound of the*
> *swift-footed horse on the frosty ground,*
> *And the horn that rang with a merry sound,*
> *and the deep-mouthed bay of the hunting hound.*
> *With the "toot-y-too" of their horn that blew,*
> *they made such a noise as on they flew*
> *That the old fox didn't know what to do ...*

Jump To It

The sport of show jumping developed nearly 100 years after steeplechasing and could be called a "new" sport, by comparison. A harness show hosted in Paris, France, in 1866 held a class for jumpers. Early jumping shows would have competitors parade in the show ring, then ride across country for the jumping portion of the contest. Because this type of show wasn't very interesting for spectators, the organizers began setting the jumps up inside the arena. These events were known not as jumping competitions, but as "lepping."

The Royal Dublin Society hosted the first official show-jumping competition in Ireland in 1864. Horses had to jump only three obstacles: a stone wall, a brush-and-rails combination, and a long jump over hurdles.

By about 1881, lepping had spread to Britain, and by 1900, most of the higher calibre shows included the classes in their program. When British military officers and regiments were stationed in Canada, they quite naturally continued the equestrian activities in which they participated at home: racing, polo, steeplechasing, and foxhunting. By 1900, these "horse games" all had a firm foothold in this country.

It seems only natural, then, that the first competition teams were made up of military men. In 1909, a Canadian team of three horse/rider combinations went to the first Nations Cup in Olympia, England. They finished in fourth place.

Until 1948, only military riders were eligible to

compete at international equestrian team events. In that year, the rule requiring competitors to be military personnel was abolished, making way for men of either "professional" or "amateur" status to compete. (Riders are considered to be professional if they are over 18 years of age and train horses for sale, give riding lessons, train or board horses, or show them for pay. Amateurs are riders over the age of 18 who do not get paid for riding or working with horses.) It was 1956 before women were allowed to ride on Olympic Nations Cup teams.

Things have changed in the past 50 years. Although there are still some military riders, who compete in uniform, the sport is dominated by civilian men and women, who compete against each other on equal terms. Oddly enough, most riders are professionals in that they give lessons or train horses to sell them, but are considered amateurs for the Olympics.

Horses and Courses

The objective of show jumping is for the horse-and-rider team to complete a course of jumps without incurring penalties by knocking down a rail or any part of the jump combinations. This takes a horse of supreme ability, one that can jump high enough to clear triple bars or parallel rails, and wide enough to cover a spread such as "stone" walls, water jumps, or combinations of any of the aforementioned obstacles.

The horse must also be fast, as there is a time limit for jumping the course. A horse/rider combination receives penalties (or faults, as they are called in the sport) if they exceed the time allowed or if the horse refuses to jump an obstacle. In addition, if they fall, or if they take the jumps in the wrong order, the horse and rider are eliminated.

When two or more horses in the same competition go clean (with no faults), they enter a "jump-off." Should they all go clean again, the winner will be the one who has completed the course in the fastest time.

In a regular jumping class there is a set number of obstacles. The horse must jump over them in a specified order, within a prescribed time limit.

However, there are almost as many kinds of jumping competitions as there are horses to enter them. In the Puissance, the goal is to see who can jump the highest. The Parcours de Chasse is a speed class, won by the fastest time. Each knockdown adds time to the final score, instead of faults. The Grand Prix tests the horses' athleticism with obstacles from four feet six inches to five feet three inches high, and spreads of six feet six inches.

Mostly, horses and riders compete as individuals. Sometimes, however, they are part of a team, often representing their country in a Nations Cup or the Olympics, and the scores of three or four horses on a team are added together. The team with the lowest score wins.

In a Scurry class, horses compete simultaneously. Two identical courses are set up and horses jump-off in heats, with the winner of each heat advancing to the next round until an overall winner is declared.

Then there are specialty jumping classes like the Gambler's Choice or the Equine/Canine Challenge held at the Royal Winter Fair in Toronto. In the Gambler's Choice, each jump is assigned a point value. The harder the jump, the more points it is worth, with the Joker fence being worth the maximum 200 points. Riders are allowed to jump the fences from either direction and in any order. They try to clear as many as they can in the allotted time of 45 seconds. The rider with the highest point total wins.

The Royal show program explains the Equine/ Canine Challenge this way: "The performing dogs are teamed up with an open jumper in this class. It is a relay race where the dogs race through their obstacles and then the horses have to negotiate their course. Both dogs and horses are timed and penalties are given for refusals and knockdowns."

No matter what type of jumping competition is

mentioned, Canadians can point with pride to the horses that carry their country's flag to the winner's circle. What follows are the unofficial biographies of just a few of the best our history has to offer.

Chapter 2
High-Flying Forefathers

High-flying horses have been a big part of Canadian history. Fantastic jumping horses set early records and made their marks for other horses to aim at. The horses whose stories are related in this chapter did not compete against each other. Their lives merely overlapped at the edges: the last years in the life of one were often the first years in the life of another.

Some of them were fine-blooded, purebred horses; others had parentage that was, to put it mildly, interesting. Some were on the show circuit for many years; others for only a few. Their lives span the years 1912 to

1971, but collectively, they reigned supreme in the show-jumping world as some of the finest examples of high-flying Canadian horses.

To Set Records, You Just Need Confidence

The year was 1912; the place, the National Horse Show in New York. Colonel Clifford Sifton (who was knighted in 1915 to become Sir Clifford) had brought his horse Confidence — piloted by Jack Hamilton, a professional rider — to the competition. Along with numerous other owners, Sifton aspired to win the title of high-jumping champion, and he had confidence in Confidence's talent.

Sifton's bay gelding was of questionable ancestry, but he was thought to be part Hackney, part who knows what. The horse was born in 1899 near Cobourg, Ontario, and eventually came into the Crowe & Murray stables in Toronto.

At a height of close to 16 hh, with a powerful, thick-set body, Confidence's action was accented by the white sock on his near hind leg. In riders' terms, he "filled the eye," and it was most likely his presence and looks that prompted a Mr. Matthews of Toronto to buy Confidence, along with a matching animal, to be used as a carriage pair.

In an ideal carriage horse, the sought-after gaits are a brisk walk, an animated yet low-speed trot, and a faster gait called the strong trot or road-trot. Cantering in harness is frowned on — but someone neglected to acquaint Confidence with this fact. When the new owner took delivery of his equine pair and put them to work, he found that Confidence "mixed his gaits" (probably meaning he cantered instead of road-trotting). Back he and his harness mate went to Crowe & Murray. Oh, the shame! Traded in for a more suitable candidate.

At the time, there were not enough heavy hunters to meet the market demand, so Jim Murray, one of the partners in the stable, resolved to test Confidence for that sector of the market. Putting the gelding over some practice fences, Murray found that Confidence had some "jump" in him, and it wasn't long before Captain W.T. Evans of Montreal bought the sturdy fellow.

While Evans owned him, Confidence was part of a team that went to the International Horse Show at Olympia, in London, England, and competed in the International Challenge Cup, featuring an award donated by King Edward VII. The event called for clearing 11 jumps in two minutes and was considered very difficult for that era. Vying for the prize against army officers from Italy and Belgium, the Canadian team, although skilful, was denied the win.

As an individual entry, however, Confidence did much better. On July 1, 1909, the *London Free Press* broadcast that Confidence had cleared a jump of seven feet, triumphing over Jubilee, a French entry, who had unsuccessfully attempted a jump of six feet eight inches. His stellar performance brought Confidence to the attention of Clifford Sifton, who promptly purchased him. Sifton also lured away Jack Hamilton, who had been the rider/horse trainer for Crowe & Murray.

No doubt this continuity in training played a large part in Confidence's future successes; in addition to being consistent winners in Canadian events, the horse/rider combination triumphed in the National Horse Show high-jump competitions in New York in both 1910 and 1911.

But it was in 1912 that Confidence's star shone brightest, for it was then, at the very same National Horse Show in New York, that he outdid himself. Each one of the competitors, in their turn, jumped their best — but their best was not good enough. Each one tried, and each one failed.

Confidence entered the ring. The crowd was focused on the bouncing bay campaigner, wondering if the obstacle would defeat him as it had done the horses that had come before him.

The rapid-fire beat of his hooves echoed as the gelding moved towards the jump. He heaved himself into the air, reaching, stretching, straining towards the rafters on his ascent to the summit of the barrier before him.

Sprightly as a deer, Confidence took to the air and sprang mightily over the top bar — and it stayed up! Not only had he outstripped all other entries, he also set the astounding record of eight feet and half an inch, a high-jump record that stood for over a decade.

It was a record not without controversy, however. An American horseman named Dick Donnelly had a horse called Heatherbloom at home on his farm in Richmond, Virginia. Donnelly claimed this horse had jumped eight feet two inches in 1902. He even had photographs of this supposed jump taking place on his farm property. But because Heatherbloom's jump hadn't been officially recorded, the mark set by Confidence remained on the books until 1923, when the American horse Great Heart jumped eight feet and thirteen-sixteenths of an inch in Chicago.

Confidence, meanwhile, had been sold to a riding school in Brooklyn, New York, in 1914, at the start of World War I. In 1915, during his stay there, Marie-Louise Thompson, who rode in a sidesaddle, took him over a seven-foot jump.

It's not uncommon for good horses to change hands often, to be bought and sold a lot. It's also not uncommon for people to buy back a horse that they've sold earlier. Perhaps the Siftons really missed their old companion, for he returned to his home at their stables a few years later. The gallant 22-year-old campaigner made a farewell appearance at the Canadian National Exhibition in 1921. In 1923, Confidence died and was laid to rest in Gormley, Ontario, on the Siftons' Foxton Farm.

The talented highflyer had lived a long life as a strong competitor with an illustrious career, staving off challenges to his supremacy for many years. He remained at the top of the heap for a period of years longer than some horses live!

Assurance in Confidence's ability as a high flyer had never been misplaced.

Air Pilot, Not for the Faint of Heart

Canada's prairie provinces are proud of their cowboy heritage, of which good, honest western horses are an unforgettable part. However, one of the most memorable horses in prairie history was not a cow pony at all, but a dynamic jumping horse named Air Pilot.

Air Pilot was a square peg in a round hole. A black Standardbred, destined by heredity and tradition to be a harness horse, he changed his destiny by the very force of his attitude and a boundless zest for competition.

He was born in 1933, during the Great Depression and in the middle of a drought, eking out an existence on not much more than Russian thistle. Despite the meagre diet, he matured into a handsome young horse and was broken for use in harness.

Unfortunately for his owners (but propitiously for him), Air Pilot was not enamoured of the standard sedate jog of a regular farm or ranch wagon horse; he wanted to race with the wind! Most farmers and ranchers of that era were more concerned with the race for survival than with racing fast horses for entertainment, but Dr. N.V. James, a veterinarian from Regina, was travelling through the area and happened to see the well-developed gelding. Dr. James was a connoisseur of fine horseflesh, so when he first glimpsed Air Pilot, he was captivated by the horse's conformation, powerful muscles, fearless manner, and above all, blazing speed. Dr. James was determined to buy this epitome of equine perfection. In 1941, $75 was a lot of money, and the former owners were convinced to part with their previously unappreciated speed-demon.

Air Pilot went into training to become a jumping horse as soon as Dr. James got him to Regina. Although he was courageous from the outset, he was quite a klutz and knocked down as many jumps as he successfully cleared. Amazingly, he never refused a jump, no matter how unlikely it was that he'd get over it. This talent was encouraging.

For every yin there's a yang, and for every silver lining there's a cloud. The cloud looming on Air Pilot's horizon was that, in spite of his admirable talent, he got fiercely impatient as soon as he saw a jumping obstacle. Immediately, the desire to jump outstripped his responsiveness to guidance from his rider. As soon as the word "go" was given, he was like a runaway locomotive hurtling towards the jump.

Despite appearances, a rider does not just go along for the ride. He or she is a vital part of the partnership, making sure the horse is at the correct take-off point to make a successful jump, neither too close to the obstacle nor too far away. The rider also tells the horse to shorten or lengthen the stride for the distances between hurdles, alerts the animal to whether they're about to scale a vertical or spread element, and guides the horse around the course to ensure he takes the jumps in the proper order.

Being Air Pilot's rider was not for the faint of heart. Because of the gelding's impetuousness, riding him was a game of chance, wavering between triumph and disaster. It was a toss-up whether he'd decide to crash through the jump or go over it.

As Air Pilot's training progressed, his jumping improved. However, no amount of training diminished the reckless abandon with which he careened around a jumping course like a demented steamroller.

He was always extremely popular with spectators because no one ever knew from one of his appearances to the next whether he would demolish the jumps, go perfectly clear, or forsake the course, jump the ringside barriers, and join them in the stands, which apparently happened on more than one occasion. Even Air Pilot himself was never sure what the day would bring — but come what may, he was consistently enthusiastic.

One might think that riding this kamikaze pony would be akin to suicide, but most of his riders — a large number of them young women — came through the experience unscathed. They had great confidence in the horse, secure in the knowledge that he might totally annihilate an obstacle, but he would never ever come to a skidding, disastrous halt or duck out before the jump.

There were a great many popular jumpers travelling the show circuit in those days. It seemed that every major city had its equine hero, and spectators at the shows were treated to battles for show-jumping supremacy between them. Brandon had Bouncing Buster, Calgary had Cool Customer, Winnipeg had Copper King ... and then, of course, there was that Pilot horse from Regina. The crowds cheered all fine performers, and Air Pilot received his share of adulation, being a fine campaigner who never disappointed his fans.

High-Flying Forefathers

Sometimes a winner, sometimes a loser, but always a sensation, Air Pilot travelled the show circuit year after year. So what if he didn't always win the show champion's trophy? Scores of show-jumping fans loved and admired his unfailing spirit and courage. They knew that if Air Pilot was on the roster, they would see a *real* show!

In the show ring, Pilot acted like a raving lunatic, as wild as the winds of a hurricane. Few people knew that once out of the limelight and back in his stall, he was a model equine citizen, gentle and quiet. All they saw was the fire and demonic tendencies he exhibited within the ring, so he never captured the level of public loyalty that some of his competitors did.

Air Pilot performed in many show rings, in towns all over the West. The best jump he ever made took place at a show in Calgary. It isn't recorded just who he was competing against, or how many other jumpers were in the class. Neither do we know if he had to complete a whole course of jumps, or whether the object of the exercise was to go for height over just one obstacle. What we can be sure of is that Air Pilot gave it his best shot, just like always. Was he fractious going into the ring? Probably. Did his rider's arms ache from the strain of trying to rein in the frenzied four-legged fury beneath him? Most likely.

Perhaps eyewitnesses to the event would have told you that Air Pilot went from a semi-controlled cavort to a nearly out-of-control bound towards the fence, with his rider clinging on like a burr. The force and speed of the horse's stride caused a wind that whipped his mane about his head in stinging tendrils. Bearing down on the barrier with vengeful purpose, Pilot's strong hind legs thrust him into the air and he rose powerfully towards the top bar. Everyone was breathless with anticipation. Come on, come on ...

Like a tornado clearing everything in its path, Air Pilot cleared the apex of the jump. He flew over the top, set at six feet four inches, and in so doing, posted a personal best height. As well, it was the highest jump ever cleared by a Saskatchewan horse.

Air Pilot was officially retired at the Calgary Horse Show in 1955. The organizers erected a jump pegged at six feet four inches to illustrate his greatest achievement. The plan was for Barney Williams, who had co-piloted the gelding over that highest jump, to ride him around the arena while the commentator explained that it was Pilot's last appearance before retiring to green pastures and a life of idle luxury. But once again, the quirky equine upset the apple cart.

At the time, Air Pilot was 22 in body, but much younger in mind. When he was ridden into the ring and saw the demonstration jump, it was all Williams could do to restrain the horse from trying to spring over it.

Four thousand spectators were on hand for the special event, and so were the top riders who had ridden Pilot at one show or another, nearly a dozen in all. While organ music swelled above his head, the "grand old man" was adorned with a wreath of flowers and received wave upon wave of applause as he took the out-gate for the last time.

Air Pilot and Dr. James, his owner, retired together on Vancouver Island, enjoying their golden years until Dr. James passed away in 1959. Shortly thereafter, Air Pilot followed, making his final flight.

Pinnacle, the High-Flying Houdini

A few horsemen have one in their barns; many don't. Those who have them, often curse them. Those who don't have them are lucky. Some owners affectionately refer to them as "characters"; others refer to them, not so affectionately, as a bloody nuisance. What are they? Equine escape artists, unofficially known as "Houdini horses."

They come in all breeds, shapes, ages, and sizes, and you never know that you have one until it's too late, and the beast is home in your barn. Be prepared: these skilful scamps can undo, untie, unlatch, or unfasten any rope, snap, button, or hook that mere humans devise.

Pinnacle, a seven-eighths Thoroughbred and high flyer extraordinaire, had an escape technique that would have done Harry Houdini proud. There was no malice in Pinnacle — he didn't do it to be bad; he just liked to have fun. Escaping was a challenge, and he couldn't resist a challenge, whether in the show ring or at home in the barn.

When Cliff Ross of Edmonton, Alberta, purchased Pinnacle in 1957, he had no idea what an eccentric equine he had acquired. Ross was simply looking for a competition horse for his daughter, Gail.

Like most professional athletes, Pinnacle was a serious and skilful competitor, but he wasn't all business. He liked to enjoy his relaxation time, too. Pinnacle was the alpha male in the Rosses' stable, and the family quickly learned his habits and preferences. His penchant for "going walkabout" was an entertaining quirk in his otherwise straightforward personality. That didn't lessen the pandemonium that ensued whenever Pinnacle took a notion into his head to liven up a quiet night among the stalls.

It was not uncommon for a stable hand to come to the barn and find that every box stall was open, and that the freed horses had made a spectacular mess. And who would, invariably, be standing in his own box stall, looking oh so nonchalant and innocent? The one responsible for the multiple breakout: Pinnacle.

The rapport that developed between Pinnacle and his rider would be the envy of any horseman. It stood them in good stead, and they racked up win after win, year after year. By 1961, the pair had competed successfully in shows all over Eastern Canada and on the fall show circuit in the U.S. as well. Even more eventfully, the accolades they received drew the attention of the Canadian Equestrian Team, and Gail Ross was selected for a place on the team — the first rider from Western Canada, as well as the first junior to achieve that distinction.

Pinnacle and his rider were so in tune with each other that they were like two halves of a whole being, a complete and cohesive unit, intimately aware of each other's strengths and weaknesses. This was no more aptly demonstrated than in 1961.

Mere days before the Canadian team was leaving to participate in an international event, Ross sustained a broken jaw, concussion, and fractured skull in a car accident. Her injuries were so grievous that doctors seriously doubted whether she would ever be able, or even want, to ride again.

Remarkably, she recovered quickly enough to be discharged from hospital only three weeks later, and began riding the stalwart Pinnacle soon afterwards. These actions speak more loudly of Pinnacle's great character than words ever could.

International show jumping is a highly competitive sport. When equestrians, especially those of international calibre, are injured, they do their darnedest to heal and get back to their chosen profession quickly. They don't want to do anything to jeopardize their chances or delay their return to the circuit, because if they're not competing, they're not in the hunt for the prize money.

Gail Ross's swift return to riding and competing was testimony that she had boundless faith in Pinnacle, trusting that he would take care of her and not cause her any further harm. Later that same year, the horse and rider won the Canadian Jumping Championship at the Royal Winter Fair. In 1963, they captured the New York Grand Prix, following a thrilling jump-off. They were also the North American open jumping champions of 1963. To top off their winning streak, they went to England, where they garnered even more prizes.

Pinnacle's exemplary career spanned 15 years, until his retirement in 1972 at the Northlands Horse Show in Edmonton. Spectators gave him a standing ovation as Gail Ross Amdam rode Pinnacle into the show ring to receive his due.

He was probably confused when, rather than directing him at some obstacles, Ross Amdam rode him to centre ring, where he was accented by a blazing spotlight. As a farewell anthem, a bugler played "The Last Post." Pinnacle was unsaddled and then covered with a horse blanket, topped off by a horseshoe-shaped wreath of roses.

Pinnacle, the high-flying Houdini, was returned to the Rosses' farm and a retirement of ease. In his career, he had travelled multiple miles, won numerous awards and titles, and, through it all, had earned a spot in the hearts of those who recognized his honesty, courage, and character.

Packaged Neatly With a Blue Beau

Puissance. The French word means "power" or "strength." The Puissance is to equestrian jumping what the pole vault is to track and field. As long as horses keep jumping "clean" (without refusals or knockdowns), officials keep raising the bar. And that's the stuff from which records are made and legends are born. One such legend was Blue Beau.

His rider, Tom Gayford, was a stockbroker by profession, but (more importantly) he was also a very competitive horseman, with a long list of achievements under his saddle. For instance, he was named

Champion Rider at the National Horse Show in 1958 and was part of the Canadian show-jumping team that wowed spectators with its riding prowess at the Royal Winter Fair in Toronto in 1960.

Blue Beau was owned by Mr. and Mrs. E. Herbert Coad of Aurora, Ontario. The Coads had loaned the talented bay gelding to the Canadian Equestrian Team, and he was paired with Tom Gayford. The two remained a competitive team for 11 years, amassing an incredible number of milestone wins during that time.

One of the most memorable moments was when they established a new Puissance world record at the National Horse Show in New York. A series of photographs in the book *Canada's International Equestrians* shows how much effort goes into breaking a world record. The six-photo sequence shows Gayford and Blue Beau throughout the execution of the jump: before, during, and after. Can you imagine what a radio announcer might have said on the momentous day, as he was describing the action?

"Ladies and gentlemen, in the ring now are Tom Gayford and his mount, Blue Beau. The jump has been raised to seven feet one inch. No one has jumped this height clean yet, but this pair will give it their best shot.

"The jump is a fake-stone wall, flanked on both sides by multi-coloured 'wings' — a formidable and intimidating obstacle in anyone's eyes. This capacity crowd is hushed, as horse and rider begin their warm-up circle ... and there they go!

"Gayford and Blue Beau race towards the jump. All we can see of Beau behind the jump is his ears. If he doesn't jump, it will be a horrible impact. There ... at the final second, Blue Beau has sprung powerfully off his hind legs — see how Gayford steadies the horse by supporting Beau's head as he lifts into the air.

"The horse is soaring over the obstacle. Gayford sits motionless, yet forward, skilfully aiding and guiding his mount while not upsetting his balance. It looks promising, folks.

"Beau snaps his front legs up tight to his belly, keeping them away from the jump. As he glides smoothly over, he extends his hind legs w-a-y back and kicks them into the air behind him as his front hooves reach the ground. With all four feet back on Mother Earth, Beau speeds away as Gayford looks back in joy and disbelief.

"Hurray! They've done it! Ladies and gentlemen, Tom Gayford and the gallant Blue Beau have triumphed in the Puissance and set a new world record of seven feet one inch here at the National Horse Show. What a night!"

New York was the scene of a series of Puissance victories for Blue Beau and Gayford. In 1960 they won, by posting a clean round three times in a row, at Madison Square Gardens. In 1961, the Puissance Wagstaff Challenge Trophy was theirs, and they assisted in a team triumph, too. It was in 1962, in repeating a Wagstaff Challenge Trophy victory, that they set the seven feet one inch Puissance record. Finally, in 1963, they won the Wagstaff for the third time, retiring the trophy.

Blue Beau's friend and rider, Tom Gayford, retired from international competition after 1968, but his expertise didn't leave the sport. He designed the show-jumping courses at the Montreal Olympics in 1976, and from 1980 through 1994 he was the Canadian team's chef d'équipe (standard industry name for a team manager). Gayford was also a member of the Canadian Equestrian Federation's national show-jumping team selection committee, and coach to his daughter, Marge Sproule.

Blue Beau continued to compete in high-flying competitions until 1965, when he was retired at the Royal Winter Fair in a special ceremony. In 1971, at the age of 23, Blue Beau died at home on the Coads' Farm in Aurora. He is buried on the farm.

Other horses jumped well, but this humble gelding always did it up fancy, with a Blue Beau.

Chapter 3
The Quest for Olympic Gold

he rules of the game are simple: jump big obstacles — lots of them. Clean. As fast as you can. Olympic show jumping is the ultimate test of a horse and rider, and nothing raises the profile of a horse/rider combination more than being able to say that they've won a medal at the Olympics.

Not many Olympic sports allow women and men to compete on equal terms, but the three equestrian disciplines — three-day eventing, dressage, and jumping — do. Moreover, the horse and rider pair are considered a team, displaying the traits of agility, daring, speed, and grace, traits that take years to perfect. At the

Olympics, feats of perfection in equestrian events often translate into gold medals.

Dressage is the supreme test of a horse's responsiveness to his rider, demanding competitors follow a set pattern of gaits and exacting movements with the rider using only the natural aids of hands, legs, and seat position to direct the horse. The Lipizzan horses of the Spanish Riding School in Austria are famous for their performances featuring many high-level dressage movements.

Three-day eventing, according to Equine Canada, "is the 'iron man' of equestrian disciplines, in which horse and rider complete three distinct tests of stamina and skill — a dressage test, a cross-country course and a stadium jumping course." A cross-country course includes two sets of roads and tracks (usually covered at a trot; the first to warm up the horse and the second as a breather between the steeplechase and cross-country), a short steeplechase course (done at a gallop over not-too-difficult jumps), and the cross-country section itself, with big, solid fences. As Equine Canada says, "A successful three-day event horse must be capable of suppleness and relaxation in the dressage test; speed, endurance and jumping ability in the cross-country course; and suppleness, obedience and energy in the stadium jumping test."

Canadian equestrians first participated in the Olympic three-day event at Helsinki in 1952, and from then on, they have never looked back.

The Road To the Medals

Team members Walter Pady, Stewart Treviranus, Tom Gayford, John Rumble, and Larry McGuinness had been training in Badminton, England, site of a famous three-day event, for six weeks before they carried the Canadian flag into Olympic equestrian battle at Helsinki.

Unfortunately, fate did not smile kindly on their high-flying endeavours. Rumble became very sick, and Pady's horse, Rocket, suffered a hock injury just after arriving in Helsinki, which meant that two of Canada's horse/rider pairs were unable to take part in the competition at all.

But the competition started off hopefully for the others. Their horses completed the first-day dressage tests competently and were passed to compete in cross-country on the second day.

The cross-country phase was no walk in the park. It included a steeplechase course that was 2.5 miles long and a cross-country course with 35 jumps in a 4.5-mile stretch. The total distance was 23 miles.

The gruelling course claimed a Canadian "victim" when Gayford, riding Constellation, came to grief at the

29th obstacle and was eliminated. McGuinness and Treviranus both completed the cross-country day without problems.

Only those who had finished the cross-country phase and had been okayed by a veterinarian could compete in the stadium jumping, held on the third day. By this time, 23 of the original 59 contestants had been eliminated. Of the 36 remaining, nine turned in clear rounds. McGuinness and Treviranus were among those nine, posting the fastest times of all: 103.6 seconds and 106.75 seconds, respectively.

Although Treviranus and McGuinness finished with no faults in both the stadium jumping and cross-country phases, neither scored high enough to be in the medals. Treviranus, riding Rustum, was ranked 22nd, while McGuinness, on Tara, was pinned in 29th place.

For the competitors — and for Canadian fans — it was a disappointing first-time showing, but better days lay ahead.

If At First You Don't Succeed ...
The world first sat up and took notice of Canadian high-jumping horses and their riders in 1956, when the Canadian team competed in the three-day event at Stockholm, Sweden. (The 1956 summer games were held in Australia, but because of the tough quarantine

rules — horses shipping in had to be kept isolated for four weeks — the equestrian events were held in Sweden.)

The road to the games began with an arduous selection process. From Regina, a young farmer named Robin Hahn applied to train with the Olympic three-day-event team. Hahn had been practically born in the saddle, riding his pony to and from school, playing horse games on the prairie, and competing in horse shows as he got older. When he was notified that the three-day-event team had accepted his application, he loaded his mare, Colette, on the back of a pickup truck and headed east.

John Rumble, who had been on the team but was too ill to compete for Canada at the Helsinki Olympics, had a young friend who he thought would make a likely candidate for the '56 team. The young man's name was Jim Elder. Rumble said Elder was "jump crazy."

Another prospective team member was Brian Herbinson, a young horseman of Irish lineage in his early 20s. The Irish have been known, down through the ages, as a "horse mad" lot, so Herbinson may have been genetically disposed to compete in the Olympic equestrian events.

When the selection was concluded, the team members were Herbinson, Rumble, and Elder, with Colonel

Charles Baker as team manager, and McGuinness as non-riding team captain. Hahn went along to help out. Horses Tara, Cilroy, and Colleen were the equine partners in the endeavour, with a horse named Steelworker as a spare.

As they had done four years earlier, the Canadians trained at the facilities in Badminton before the competition. This proved beneficial, especially to Cilroy, who had been prone to rush his jumps. The training period taught him to slow down and be more cautious. The Olympic team horses and riders even competed in a one-day event at Sherborne, Dorset, before leaving for the Olympics.

In the van on the way to the airport prior to their flight to Stockholm, Cilroy was hurt. He had a cut above his hock, which became bruised and hugely swollen. The team was very concerned about the injury, not only for the horse's sake, but also because no changes in mount were allowed after a horse had been declared for the competition. If a horse or rider became sick or injured, the team would be disqualified. Fortunately, Cilroy recovered enough to pass the veterinary check and was allowed to start.

Unbelievable Hurdles
The men and horses had trained hard, and between

them they had countless years of experience in the jumping field. Despite all their training and experience, though, they couldn't believe the size and composition of the Olympic cross-country course. Oil drums, tables, chairs, umbrellas — all were employed in jump construction, combined with wide spreads and tall jumps guaranteed to tax the skill of both horse and rider to the utmost. One example that gives an indication of the severity of the course was the log jump. A horse negotiating this jump would drop four feet into water, which was two feet deep, then had to scale another wall, four feet high, to get back out. And there were 33 of these unbelievable hurdles in all.

The day of the cross-country competition, it poured rain. In spite of the inclement weather and the almost-insurmountable obstacles, the Canadians persevered, and their perseverance was rewarded. They earned a bronze medal and came home to Canada to a hero's welcome.

They were greeted at the airport by a crowd of enthusiastic supporters, and Canadian newspapers printed banner headlines about the win. Major General and Mrs. C.C. Mann — who at one time owned the famous Joker's Hill farm near King, Ontario — hosted a gala dinner party in their honour. The dinner menus were illustrated with head studies of Colleen, Tara, and

Cilroy engraved under the Olympic rings, and the menu items were named for the cross-country obstacles.

All of Canada was proud of the Olympic high flyers, and dedicated Canadian equestrians looked forward to the next set of games, where they might have their chance at Olympic glory.

Stables and Stars

What do a curvaceous movie star and a Canadian jumping horse have in common? In 1959, they both did their bit to promote the participation of a Canadian team in the Rome Olympics of 1960.

The horse was Roma, the big brown gelding designated to be Brian Herbinson's mount in Rome. The actress was Gina Lollobrigida, the alluring female lead of many a silver-screen epic. Ms. Lollobrigida, who was living in Toronto at the time, was asked if she would sponsor a new horse on the Canadian Olympic team, and she graciously obliged. Stacks of photos were taken of the athletic horse and beautiful actress, and newspaper editors everywhere ate the publicity stunt up. (It is not recorded anywhere how Roma felt about the media circus, nor if he was invited to attend the party Ms. Lollobrigida hosted for the team after the Olympics were over.)

Olympic Disaster

If you were to ask a cross-country competitor to describe the three-day event at the Rome Olympics of 1960 in one word, he or she would probably say "Disastrous!"

Brian Herbinson, Jim Elder, Norman Elder, and Tom Gayford were the riders faced with guiding, encouraging, and even babying the horses Roma, Canadian Envoy, Royal Beaver, and Pepper Knowes around the punishing course.

The altitude and heat combined to take a toll on riders and horses from every team that participated. Later on, Jim Elder said that the carnage among horses and riders during the cross-country phase of the Rome three-day event was "so appalling that authorities seriously considered removing future Three-Day Events from Olympic competitions." Although Elder also maintained that the jumps in Rome were not more difficult than those at Stockholm, he did say that, due to poor planning and construction, they were definitely more perilous. Solid timber had been used to construct the jumps in Sweden, but the obstacles on the course in Rome were composed of thin, easily broken tree trunks, sewer piping, and other less than stout material. In addition, the approaches to and landing areas after the jumps were sub-standard. This was proven when

Norman Elder and his mount fell at the second fence due to the sand on the landing side giving way.

The round endured by Pepper Knowes and Tom Gayford was a like a bad dream that keeps repeating and repeating. At a water obstacle, the horse fell and was completely covered by water. The only thing that saved him from drowning before help could arrive was Gayford's holding the horse's head above water. After the aquatic rescue, Gayford remounted and the pair carried on to the next jump, a woodpile, where the horse fell again. Somehow, a splinter of wood was driven into the horse's foot in such a way as to paralyse the injured leg. The Canadian team's veterinarian anesthetized the horse and removed the wood, with instantaneous results: the leg was sound again.

The horses were worn out by the mountainous terrain of the roads and tracks portion even before the cross-country phase started. The number of disqualified entrants ballooned upwards as horses and riders fell all over the course. Ambulances and even helicopters were needed in some of the rescues. Jim Elder described the area as being like a battlefield. Norman Elder happened upon one rider lying in the grass, having a heart attack. Gillian Wilson (owner of Pepper Knowes) was lunching in a tent with some friends. When she left, she found a horse lying dead outside.

Fortunately, neither the men nor the horses of the Canadian Olympic team suffered any lasting injury. Jim Elder and his mount, Canadian Envoy, were the only Canadian combination to finish the course, which garnered them an individual 10th place. However, the team was eliminated because other members were unable to finish.

"The presence of friends and members of their families didn't make up for the disappointments and frustrations," writes Zita Barbara May in her book *Canada's International Equestrians.* "It was generally agreed that 'Rome was a disaster'."

Perhaps the one good thing that came out of the Rome disaster was new and improved rules for designing cross-country courses.

Guts and Glory in Mexico
In 1968, after their high flyers sat out the previous Olympic Games, the people of Canada pinned their hopes on their "best of the best." They sent a show-jumping team to Mexico City, a team which included two men who had previously competed in Olympic three-day events: Jim Day on Canadian Club, Tom Gayford aboard Big Dee, and Jim Elder on The Immigrant. Terrance "Torchy" Millar and his mount, Beefeater, went to the games as a spare combination.

Captain Tom

Tom Gayford, stockbroker and avid horseman, had come by his love of riding honestly. He was the son of Colonel Gordon Gayford, an intense supporter of the Toronto and North York Hunt, who had also been a member of the Canadian team during international competitions.

Tom had accumulated an impressive array of honours, starting in the late 1940s when he began his riding career. A strong competitor, and a force to be reckoned with, Gayford and his mounts had posted numerous wins in both hunter and jumper events.

Gayford had been selected as part of the Canadian three-day event team for the 1956 Olympics, but decided he should stay at home because of business considerations. He continued to compete across North America in succeeding years in both show jumping and three-day events, and posted some of his most notable wins between 1956 and 1965, including three times winning the Puissance Wagstaff Challenge competition at the National Horse Show in New York with the incomparable Blue Beau.

When Gayford had the opportunity to attend the Mexico Olympics as part of the Canadian show-jumping team, he leapt at the chance and was chosen team captain.

Jim the Elder, Jim the Younger

Jim Elder's family farm north of Toronto was the scene of his first forays into the riding and jumping world. Elder joined the Canadian Equestrian Team in the 1950s, when he was chosen as a replacement after one of the team riders got sick. "Since they had some small horses left and I was a small guy, I got to go," Elder explained in a 1999 interview for CBC Sports Online.

Elder's self-depreciating comment made it sound like his participation with the team was a case of being in the right place at the right time, but in fact he possessed phenomenal riding ability. The talented horseman helped win a team bronze medal in the three-day event at the 1956 Stockholm Olympics, as well as numerous Pan-American Games medals. He competed regularly in both show jumping and three-day eventing.

Jim Day lived just the next farm over from Jim Elder and was an enthusiastic horseman from childhood. (His first mount was a little donkey named Buttermilk.) He often would ride across the back fields and jump the fence to get to Elder's farm, where the elder Jim would give riding advice to the younger Jim. Day's riding ability impressed Elder. "Jimmy Day was an exceptional rider," Elder continued in the same CBC interview. "He was like the Bobby Hull or Bobby Orr of jumping. He had talent oozing out."

Day began his equestrian career in 1964, when he was only 18 years of age. His performance at the International Junior Horse Show, held north of Toronto in Cedar Valley, earned him the title of North American Junior Jumping Champion, and he was selected for the Canadian show-jumping team.

Tough Timber

The jumping course in Mexico City was declared one of the toughest Olympic courses ever built, with 17 large fences set close together and at awkward angles. "They hired a Dutch course designer. They gave him the dimensions of the stadium and he designed it on paper," Elder later explained. "They neglected to tell him that at least 30 feet were needed on either side for the track and field. It shortened up the whole stadium, the whole ring. Instead of putting jumps where the designer wanted, they had to shorten them all, to smaller and different distances."

Team show jumping was the final event on the last day of the games. Germany, France, Great Britain, the United States, and Australia had all fielded strong teams. The Canadian team was relatively new, internationally, and the team riders were "virtually unknown," but at the start of the second round, they were close behind France in first place.

Hopes were high that the equestrian team could break the jinx that seemed to be plaguing Canadian athletes at these games. Up to this point, Canada had won only four medals in all disciplines, and there were no gold medals in the collection.

Big Dee, Big Mare for a Big Job

Team captain Gayford was the first Canadian to ride, on a mare called Big Dee, an also-ran from the racetrack, that became an Olympic star. Sired by Unsinatus, an imported grandson of Nearco, the 17 hh brown mare was bought as a four-year-old off the Fort Erie track by Tom Gayford and his father, Gordon, in 1963.

They paid a paltry $400 for her, and for the first year she was used as a mount in the Toronto and North York Hunt. Gordon Gayford found that although she could be careless over low jumps, Big Dee improved when put to large fences. It wasn't long before she said her last good-byes to the hunting field: Tom Gayford snapped her up as a hot Olympic prospect.

Prior to the games, Big Dee had distinguished herself by helping the Canadian team win a bronze medal in the show-jumping competition at the 1967 Pan-American Games in Winnipeg. With this accolade under her girth, Gayford set his sights on higher aspirations and felt that Big Dee was a mare who could do the job.

At the '68 Olympics, she proved that she could.

"I had a little more experience, and once I got around [the course], I could come back and say, 'Okay, watch that corner down there, it's tough getting into that combination, and the time is tight'," explained Gayford in a 1999 interview for *The Olympians*, found at CBC-TV Online. "I went in there and the next guy knew exactly what to do and where I lost it."

Canadian Club

The next Canadian team member to ride was Jim Day, on Canadian Club. Another horse bought off the track, the chestnut Thoroughbred, standing 16.3 hh, became an exceptional jumper and went on to record impressive wins throughout his career. He attacked jumping courses with bravery, power, and boldness.

He began his career in Florida in 1966, claiming the title of Champion of the Circuit. In Harrisburg, Pennsylvania, on the fall circuit, he jumped six feet nine inches, and later, at the National Horse Show in New York, he flew over the bar at seven feet one inch.

In the year prior to the Olympics, Canadian Club and Jim Day competed in the Winnipeg Pan-Am Games, on the same team as Gayford and Elder. This spring-loaded horse earned an individual gold medal for jumping. He leaped a height of seven feet three inches, setting a Puissance record in the process. He was deemed to be one of the greatest Canadian-bred horses of the era.

Canadian Club thrived on competition, and in Mexico he gave Day an excellent ride, posting only 12 faults. This turned up the heat on the French team's final rider. If he posted a good round, Canada's hopes for a gold would be dashed. But the Canadian team still had its "ace in the hole" with Jim Elder and The Immigrant.

The Immigrant, Olympic Rodeo Star

All horse enthusiasts, whether they own their own equines or simply love them from afar, have a favourite. Sometimes a horse is loved for his ability, sometimes for a facet of his character, such as his attitude or simply because he returns the love lavished on him by his owner.

The Immigrant was a horse with an incredible jumping capability, which garnered him many fans. But what really seemed to grab people was his propensity for misbehaviour under saddle. The talented high flyer couldn't keep his feet on the ground, even between the jumps. It was nothing for him to flourish his heels in the air after a jump, making the job of piloting him akin to riding a bucking bronco at the Calgary Stampede. It is amazing that a horse with such unorthodox style turned into an Olympic star.

Bob Ballard originally bought The Immigrant from a member of the Ox Ridge Hunt in Darien, Connecticut. Ballard then turned around and sold the horse to former Olympic skater Bill McLachlan as a prospect for the show-jumping circuit. Knowing that McLachlan didn't plan to ride the horse himself, Ballard suggested that Jim Elder might be interested in taking the mount. (Many riders don't own their own horses, but instead ride animals owned by people who love horses and jumping competitions and want to take part in the excitement of showing, but who don't ride themselves, or have bought the horse as an investment. These people buy horses and donate them for use by the Canadian team.)

In 1968, The Immigrant was still a young horse, and crowds sometimes excited him. He got plenty of excitement at the Olympics. It took all of Elder's skill to maintain the equilibrium of both his horse and himself. "When you're standing there and coming down the ramp and the crowd, the feeling of the crowd in the big Olympic stadium, it's really quite a feeling," recalled Elder for the CBC *Olympians* interview. "The horse feels it too, you could just feel his heart. It was pounding about a hundred miles an hour."

The last rider for the French team went just before Elder. Unfortunately, the stress of competition got to both the Frenchman and his mount, and their final score was a whopping 28 faults. Suddenly Canada was back in the chase for the gold, and it all hinged on Jim Elder and The Immigrant.

Horse and rider bounded over the first six obstacles and left them standing. So far, so good. But at the seventh obstacle, The Immigrant's leg brushed a rail, and down it went. With intense concentration and skill — and a good dose of luck — the pair was able to finish the course with no other faults. Final score: Canada, 102.75 faults; France, 110.50 faults; and Germany, 117.25 faults.

Won By a Whisker

When all the horses had completed the course and the points were tallied, the Canadians had won the gold medal by the slimmest of margins — a mere 7.75 faults. The jubilant team members performed their victory gallop before packed stands. The glow of their accomplishment was rivalled only by the shine of Canada's first and only gold medal of the Mexico Olympics.

The members of the 1968 Olympic team surmounted a string of obstacles, both in getting to the prestigious event and at the event itself. They pulled off one of the most exciting upset wins in Olympic history.

Chapter 4
Barra Lad: Four-Legged Dynamite

art Hackney, part Standardbred. One breed known for its high-stepping, showy gait; the other for its speed on the racetrack. Not, by any stretch of the imagination, a cross that any knowledgeable horseman would purposely choose in an effort to breed a prospective jumping horse. But in Barra Lad's case, it resulted in one of the most spectacular high-flying jumping horses of all time. He was like four-legged dynamite, exploding over jumps.

The Horse
Essondale, near Coquitlam, British Columbia, was the

location of Colony Farm, an experimental farm facility that gained international recognition for breeding top-quality Holstein cows. It seems incongruous that a strangely bred foal like Barra Lad ended up there, but he was simply the result of a "Hey, baby, I've jumped the fence and no one's looking" unplanned liaison between his Hackney father and Standardbred-type mother. In any event, Barra Lad was born in 1918, and since his dam died shortly after his birth, he required human intervention and bottle-feeding to survive.

As orphan foals are prone to do, he became more than a little spoiled. Naturally, he viewed his human nursemaids as surrogate mothers, and as he was so friendly, he quickly became a favourite of the farm workers.

It is easy to picture him in the mind's eye: impossibly long-legged and awkward, with a fuzzy foal face, and that whisk-broom tail flapping like a windshield wiper as he prances about the farm, poking his white-blazed muzzle into places it doesn't belong and generally making a nuisance of himself. Oh, see him now! There he is, over at the clothesline. Look at that little imp, his bright, intelligent eyes dancing with mischief as he grabs a freshly washed bedsheet in his teeth. He tugs at it until, snip-snap, the clothespins zing free and away he races, the sheet billowing about his ears and trailing out behind him like an oversized, tailless kite.

Unfortunately, cute tricks can quickly turn into annoying habits, and the little orphan prince's freedom to roam the farm was curtailed shortly after his escapades became too much to endure. Time passed and he grew into a sterling example of teenage horse-hood. The fuzzy colt became a strapping bay horse, solid of muscle, shiny of coat, with unblemished confirmation, keen intelligence, and a captivating disposition.

As the young prince grew, he began to show a pre-disposition to jump whatever got in his way. He would much rather go *over* obstacles in his path than go around them. It was not unusual for Bill McVee, the farm superintendent, to visit the colt's paddock only to find that the impudent upstart had pulled a Harry Houdini act, escaped the confines of his corral, and was unconcernedly grazing where the grass was always greener.

Naturally, the fences were built higher after each breakout, but their efforts to contain the rascal were fruitless; no matter how high the fences were built, he jumped over them.

The Man

While the orphan colt was growing up in BC, the man who would play an important part in his destiny was establishing himself 700 kilometres away in Calgary. That man was Peter Welsh.

Welsh was a Scotsman who had emigrated from the Old Country in the early 1900s. A canny soul, he had numerous children and even more numerous business ideas. Little information can be found about Welsh before he left his homeland; however, his coups in Canada are countless.

Welsh set about building an empire in his new home. One of its most notable elements was the Calgary Sales Repository, among the first livery stables in the city of Calgary. His success was due in large part to the fact that Welsh had a keen eye for a horse and was known as one of the finest judges of horseflesh in Canada in his time. The Canadian Pacific Railway hired him to buy horses for settlers coming to new farms under CPR's land settlement plan. This gave Welsh the opportunity to search for fine horses for himself as well, and he gained a reputation as quite a horse trader. Horses were his business, but high jumpers were his passion. He set his sights on having a stable full of the best high-jumping horses and went about accomplishing that goal.

Welsh had seven children — Alphie, Cathy, John, Josie, Mary, Louis, and Peter. Most of them were given riding lessons practically before they could walk, although Mary was terrified of horses and never rode. Their ambitious father soon had them competing in horse shows. He became a trophy hunter, and as the children racked up more and more wins, they also developed a string of talented jumping horses second to none.

Welsh's stable of high-flying horses and fearless young riders became renowned throughout the horse-show circuit. Crowds flocked to see their performances. Horse shows were notorious for running late into the night; nevertheless, loyal fans waited sometimes as late as 3:00 am to watch the Welsh children display their prowess. Little Alphie Welsh was an especial favourite, piloting an elegant, dock-tailed grey mare called Mademoiselle.

Once Welsh achieved his dream of owning the best horses in Canada, he immediately pressed on towards another goal, seeking even higher acclaim: he wanted to own a world champion high jumper.

The Partnership

Horsemen like to brag about their horses. So, in the spring of 1921, when Bill McVee mentioned to Welsh that there was a colt at home in BC that could jump out of any field they put him in, Welsh lost no time in deciding to buy the horse. He offered $150 (equivalent to about $1300 today) without even seeing the animal. What faith! What optimism! What a fortuitous deal for Welsh.

When the young prince arrived at his new home, he was given the official show name Barra Lad, in honour of Mrs. Welsh's Scottish birthplace. He was stabled with Mademoiselle, and the two animals became fast friends. They were so close that it seemed as if Barra Lad, the orphan foal, had found a new mother, and Mademoiselle had found a new child. They disliked being separated from each other, and during Barra Lad's future jumping competitions, the grey mare had to be brought into the ring in order to calm him down.

Barra Lad was put into training with Louis and Josie Welsh, Peter's two eldest sons. It was between the Lad and Louis that a special rapport developed. Louis had the gift of "horseman's hands" — quiet, kind, guiding, and supportive. Barra Lad responded to Louis with the gifts that great horses give their riders: affection and a willingness to give their all.

Under the boys' tutelage, the Lad blossomed, his abilities increased, and Peter Welsh decided to take the three-year-old wonder horse east to test his mettle and see how he stacked up against the "big names" in the show ring of the day. When he began triumphing over experienced veterans of jumping competitions from the

Atlantic to the Pacific, the Welsh family horsemen discovered they had a real champion in their possession.

The Challenge

Imagine how it would feel to try and jump over an obstacle that is higher than you are tall. You can't see what's on the other side, so it's a jump into the unknown, pure and simple — equivalent to closing your eyes and walking off the edge of a cliff.

Horses chasing the high-jump record face this challenge repeatedly. Yet, time after time, they thunder powerfully towards a jump and propel themselves into the air ... up, up, up! ... in an effort to clear the opponent obstacle. To fail means disqualification at best, serious injury at worst. But Barra Lad met the challenge over and over again.

Following his success with the Calgary Sales Repository, Peter Welsh had yet another brain wave: Why not start a travelling rodeo show? And so, the Alberta Stampede Company was born, with Welsh's stable of high jumpers as the main attraction in addition to the rodeo acts on the bill.

People were fascinated by Barra Lad's jumping prowess and eccentric disposition. Gentle and friendly to work around in his stall, he was the epitome of an ideal mount. Who could ever imagine that this mellow

Barra Lad: Four-Legged Dynamite

Louis Welsh, aged 15, jumping Barra Lad in 1923.

creature, ambling down the side of a sun-dappled country road on a fine summer day, as meek and gentle as an old stable hack for hire, had an aberration? But he had the equine equivalent of a Jekyll-and-Hyde personality. As soon as a rider brought him into the show ring and pointed him at a jump, Barra Lad turned into a snorting, fire-breathing monster.

"It's hard to explain," Louis Welsh said in an interview in the Summer 1977 edition of *Golden West* magazine. "He could be so gentle and quiet, but when he got in the ring he got so excited we couldn't hold him. I've seen two men try to hold him and two men try to get me on top. He'd kick and bite, but I wasn't afraid of him."

Higher and Higher

In 1922, at the Brandon Spring Show, Barra Lad wowed the crowd by establishing a Manitoba record when he leaped over the bars set at 6 feet 10 inches on the Monday night of the show. Only three days later, he blasted his own previous record off the books, surpassing it by an amazing three inches when he cleared the height of seven feet one inch.

Between 1922 and 1925, Barra Lad's amazing leaps continued to dominate the high-jump statistics. For seven consecutive days, he performed and cleared the seven-foot mark at a huge show in Seattle, Washington. Following his triumphs in Seattle, the Lad was taken back home to Calgary, where, on April 1, 1925, he played to the home crowd with gusto for the final time, jumping a bar set at seven feet one inch. Scarcely six months later, Barra Lad reached the pinnacle of his career, not at home in Calgary, but in New Westminster, BC.

The great horse's fame was such that, on the night of his record-breaking jump, the host arena — designed to hold 6000 people — was bursting at the seams. Spectators streamed in, ticket sellers were kept on the hop, and the building's balconies, one above the other, were in danger of collapsing from the weight of all the eager high-jump aficionados. The building inspector and fire marshal were trying to stop ticket sales and eject a number of the people who were already in the stands, but others kept piling in.

On this auspicious occasion, the official measuring was being done by two Supreme Court judges. Fred Kennedy, a newspaper reporter and Welsh's publicity director, was in the ring as well. Josie and Fred Welsh were in position at either side of the obstacle. If horse or rider got into trouble, it was their job to release the top bars. (Archival photographs of Barra Lad and other horses in high-jump competitions show a jumping structure shaped like a flat-bottomed U. The sides of the U form an alleyway, which the horse enters on his way to the obstacle. The jump itself consists of a number of poles parallel to the ground; in some of the photos, the upper poles are tied or held onto the corner uprights, which are set into the ground. In others, the parallel poles are only on the upper half of the jump; the lower half is piled with what appears to be cut brush.)

Although Barra Lad had come into the arena with an uncharacteristically quiet demeanour, when he began to pick up the frenzied vibes of the swelling crowd, he started getting excited himself.

He warmed up by frisking over a jump set at six feet. The bars were raised, and he then faced up to the seven-foot jump, floating over as lightly as thistledown drifts on a summer breeze. At that point, Fred Kennedy made an announcement that silenced the crowd: the champion would attempt to clear 8 feet 1.5 inches and set a world high-jumping record.

Everyone was focussed on Barra Lad and his youthful rider as they walked up to the jump and stood there looking at it. "Usually I'd never do that with him," Louis said in an interview years later, "because he'd have gone right through it."

Just as carefully, Louis guided his horse back to the starting point. Then he turned Barra Lad around and the horse accelerated towards the jump. At the last minute, without warning, the Lad stopped dead and ducked sideways, bumping some of the lower poles, which were loosely stacked on the jump. Louis yelled at the attendants and judges to hurry and get the poles back in place: he could feel his horse reaching the point of no return — he was ready to give the jump a try.

Again Louis took the champion back to the end of the ring. The starter waved the flag, and, responding to the urging of his rider's hands and voice, the exuberant horse raced towards the jump, with Louis flattened low over his neck.

With seemingly effortless strides, Barra Lad bore down on the obstacle and then, at its very base, he sprang powerfully off his haunches and bounded into the air, as a partridge flushed by a hunter bursts out of the brush to freedom in the sky.

Time slowed and seemed to stop as he cleaved the air on his way to the summit of the jump. Such was the power and scope of his leap that his front legs cleared the bar by a good six inches; however, his hindquarters were trailing out behind him, and he looked to be in danger of knocking the whole obstacle down. At the last second, the valiant warrior tucked his hind legs up, too, and in an instant, with almost unbelievable power, surged over the top and descended the other side.

The force of his trajectory was so great that he was unable to land normally on his front feet. Instead, he stumbled to his knees. Because his neck was still outstretched, his muzzle dug a large groove in the dirt of the arena floor. He scrambled to his feet amid exultant cheers and thunderous applause. He had done it! Barra Lad, a true Canadian hero, had set a world record with a mark of 8 feet 1.5 inches.

The crowd went wild, swarming down into the ring and surrounding the champion, eager to pat him and congratulate his rider. In the same manner that the Kentucky Derby winner is awarded a wreath of flowers, Barra Lad's neck was adorned with a floral horseshoe, and the riotous strains of "There'll Be a Hot Time in the Old Town Tonight" blared through the building as the band swung into action.

There was such a crush that police were required to control the crowd so the hero could be returned to the barn. After he was cooled down, Barra Lad was tucked up in his stall and given his feed.

The Aftermath
Long into the night, Peter Welsh, his family, and cohorts discussed Barra Lad's future. Ideas for new records to attempt flew fast and furious. There was even a Hollywood movie to be made. Finally, the Welshes retired for a few hours of sleep. An early morning loomed, as the whole shebang — riders and horses — was due at the county fair in Puyallup, Washington. But morning began even earlier than anticipated.

Peter Welsh was jerked from slumber by the strident ring of the phone. The call summoned him to the barn: Barra Lad was sick! Welsh woke Kennedy, and they lost no time in getting to the stable, where groom Pat Young gave them sombre news. Barra Lad, usually eager for his mash, hadn't touched it. Even worse, he had suddenly lowered his head, falling face first into a corner of the stall, injuring himself above the eyes.

Doctors Agar and Black, government veterinarians, got the horse up and into the barn alleyway and commenced working on him. By this time, Barra Lad was bleeding from the mouth; the vets suspected internal hemorrhaging.

The vets worked feverishly as, all around them, preparations were being made to load horses, tack, and equipment on the train nearby. One by one the horses were led away. The last to go was Barra Lad's closest companion, the grey mare Mademoiselle. She had become increasingly upset as the drama unfolded and was reluctant to leave her stricken stablemate, but finally, after stopping to gently nose him and nicker, she too was led away.

Shortly thereafter, with none of the fanfare that heralded his life, Barra Lad quietly died.

The Record That Wasn't
The scene of Barra Lad's greatest triumph became that of his greatest tragedy. He was buried on the grounds of the arena, with his horseshoe victory wreath, by now withered, the only marker of his final resting place.

The autopsy done after Barra Lad died showed that the main artery leading to his liver had been ruptured, resulting in the hemorrhage. Louis Welsh thought that the shock of the jump and landing was to blame. "It's too high for any horse; they can't reach the ground," he told the interviewer from *Golden West* magazine in 1977. "You know it's foolishness when you start jumping like that. It's crazy."

Sadly, that world record jump was never recognized by the *Guinness Book of Records*. In fact, Barra Lad's name is not mentioned in that tome at all. The Welsh family was so overwhelmed by the unexpectedness of Barra Lad's tragic death that no one gave a thought to notifying the authorities at Guinness of the new record. Captain A. Larraguibel Morales and his mount, Huasó, are listed as the official high-jump champions, with a record of 2.47 metres (8 feet 1.25 inches) in Santiago, Chile, on February 5, 1949.

Today, no statue marks the burial site of Canada's greatest jumping horse. The arena in which he set the record was destroyed by fire over 30 years ago. Aside from a handful of photographs in the Glenbow Foundation archives, a few magazine articles, and a chapter in Grant MacEwan's book *Memory Meadows*, Barra Lad has been almost forgotten.

But in the imagination of those who aspire to surpass his record, he lives on: one of the greatest high flyers of them all.

Chapter 5
Equine Quirks

Any horseman worth his or her oats will tell you that, like humans, no two horses are exactly the same. When put to work, a properly trained horse will, for the most part, always do his best to accomplish the task you've asked of him. Horsemen have a term for this trait: they call it "honesty."

However, a horse can be as honest as the day is long and still have idiosyncrasies. Perhaps a draft horse works better if he is harnessed on the right side of the team harness, rather than the left. Perhaps the racing Thoroughbred will refuse to be led into the horse trailer, but will walk in quietly by himself, with the end of the lead shank merely thrown over his withers. There are probably as many different equine quirks as there are different equines!

The horses in this chapter were all high-flying stars in their own right, but in addition, they all had unusual eccentricities that added excitement to the lives of their owners and fans.

Montreal, The Reluctant Competitor

Canadian equestrians have a long history of competing — and winning — at Madison Square Gardens in New York City. The November 12, 1929, issue of the *Toronto Mail and Empire* featured a photo of Lieutenant C.C. Mann and his mount Montreal. The pair had won the trophy for the international military stake at the Gardens, besting 30 other riders from five countries.

The majority of show-jumping horses are eager to compete in the show ring. While Montreal was an excellent jumping horse, what made him noteworthy was not his ability as a high flyer, but rather his reticence about entering the ring at this particular show. He was so unenthusiastic that it was laughable.

According to Zita Barbara May, Lieutenant Mann and Montreal were waiting their turn at ringside. Mann prepared to mount just as the announcer heralded their arrival in the ring. The announcement startled Montreal and he jerked back, snapped a rein, and broke free. He decamped at high speed, back to his stall; Lieutenant Mann was ingloriously left behind on the ground.

The National Horse Show had used and appreciated the expert announcing services of Otis Trowbridge for a number of years, and he and his audiences enjoyed a longstanding camaraderie. Trowbridge apparently decided to milk this disappearing horse act for all it was worth.

While another competitor rode in Lieutenant Mann's place, Trowbridge, with counterfeit consternation, apologized for his "mistake." Montreal was fetched back to ringside, wearing a new, strong bridle that the harried grooms had found and hastily substituted for the broken one.

Trowbridge again announced, "Lieutenant C.C. Mann on Montreal," having seen them appear at ringside to await their chance to compete. It was déjà vu. The announcement was accompanied by the sound of reverberating hoofbeats. Montreal again fled, this time leaving his whole bridle behind as he sought the safety of his home away from home. In mock sorrow, Trowbridge broadcast to the crowd that he had gotten it wrong again and introduced another rider instead.

The Canadian team's aggravated officials deserved full points for perseverance. The groom, with the recalcitrant Montreal in tow, was directed to lead the horse into the ring and allow Mann to mount the horse inside the gate.

These antics caused the announcer to pretend that he was mightily embarrassed by his previous announcing errors. "Ladies and gentlemen," Trowbridge shouted, "I crave your forgiveness ... called it wrong again! Lieutenant C.C. Mann, Canada, *with* Montreal!"

At this point, Lieutenant Mann's groom, discomfited by the circus-like events, gave the rider such a powerful boost up into the saddle that Mann's momentum carried him right over Montreal's back and down onto the arena floor again. The building resounded with chortles and guffaws.

Mann finally succeeded in mounting the bashful Montreal, and the horse sprang over the jumps with enough skill and panache to win the $1000 Military Jumping Stake.

Poor Montreal. How ironic that the jumping star should be so introverted when he shared a name with Montreal, a city known for its extroverted inhabitants.

Michael, Horse of Iron

Just imagine the consternation and outrage that would erupt today among show-jumping competitors if they were asked to go back into the ring and repeat their jumping round, over and over and over!

Modern competitions commonly consist of two rounds, followed by a jump-off to break any ties. However, prior to 1949, when the "one jump-off, fewest faults, fastest time" method of determining winners was adopted, Canadian show-jumping competitions involved multiple jump-offs. The horses kept going round the whole course until one emerged with the fewest — or no — faults. Quite naturally, horses with the strongest constitution and in the best condition usually captured the prize.

Michael had been purchased in the early 1920s by Colonel R.S. McLaughlin of Oshawa, Ontario, who wanted a mannerly horse for his own use. McLaughlin ordered his daughter Eleanor not to touch the horse, but she sneaked him out of the stable to test his jumping ability — which she found to be terrific.

When he found out about this direct violation of his edict, her father was incensed, but when he calmed down, he made Eleanor a gift of Michael. The young lady and her horse began entering — and winning — horse shows, which set the stage for Michael's appearance with C.C. Mann (Eleanor's husband) at the Royal of 1932.

In the first go-round, Michael and 31 other horses navigated the prescribed course, which included a gate (set at four feet six inches), a stone gate (four feet eight inches), and a triple jump (three elements ranging from 4 feet 10 inches to five feet two inches). Nine of the horses had no faults.

The second round of jumping pared that number down to four. By the fifth jump-off there were only two competitors in the running: Roxana and Michael.

A jump-off is an arduous experience for any horse. To be included, they've already gone around the course twice, with no faults. Make no mistake, by the end of the second round, most horse are tired! The jump-off, in which they must again go clean, as well as faster than any other horse in order to win, can be exhausting. So just imagine how these final two competitors felt, as each entered the ring for the fifth time ...

Roxana went first and sailed around the course perfectly — until the last jump, where she bumped a top rail off. Michael alone was left in the running. Could he do it?

He did! The horse with the seemingly iron constitution whisked around the course one last time, leaving every obstacle standing and posting yet another clear round. He had cleared 40 jumps since the start of the class and more than deserved the silver trophy he won.

Equine Quirks

Roger II, From Buggy to Bounder

If the brown gelding named Roger II had been more amenable and not earned a reputation as a rogue in harness, he might never have found his true calling and won the prestigious President of Mexico's Trophy at the Royal Winter Fair Horse Show in 1949.

In that competition, for the first time, the Royal adopted the standardized rules of the Fédération Equestre Internationale (International Equestrian Federation). Up until then, the Royal — and other Canadian horse shows — scored jumping competitions by using "slats" — thin slips of wood placed along the tops of jumps, which, when dislodged, counted as faults against the horse.

These slats caused enormous kerfuffle at shows. A horse received four faults if he knocked slats off with his front legs, but only two faults if he hit them with his hind. This made score-keeping a nightmare for the officials, as they had to decide if the slats had been disturbed when the horse was going up or coming down. As well, there was no time limit to the classes; rather, jump-offs were used to determine a winner in the event of a tie score. If there were several good jumpers in a class, the jump-offs just kept going on and on, sometimes all night.

By 1949, 37 countries had adopted the FEI rules,

which used the "least amount of faults in the fastest time" method. FEI officials were receiving complaints from international team riders about the Canadian show rules, and they soon dictated that international teams would no longer compete at the Royal if the show did not join the FEI. Despite objections (in some cases quite vehement) from Canadian officials and riders alike, the Canadian Horse Shows Association adopted the FEI rules, but the Royal Winter Fair refused.

However, the Royal did schedule a special jumping competition on the last night of the 1949 fair, which would use the FEI rules. It was also the first time in Canada that members of international military teams and civilians competed together. The President of Mexico donated a trophy for the winner.

Fifteen extremely colourful jumps were set up in the ring, to the horror of a number of horses that balked at going over them. The rainbow-coloured obstacles didn't faze Roger II — he was game to jump anything. He loved to jump!

A Mennonite farmer in Hamburg, Ontario, had acquired the bounding bay gelding as a showy candidate to pull his buggy to church, but Roger had higher aspirations than being a harness horse. All the other horses stood patiently, quietly waiting until the service was over. Not Roger. He got bored, kicked the buggy into firewood, shucked off his bridle, nonchalantly scaled the fence, and lit out for the comforts of home. He also had a propensity for escaping from the pasture, clearing the five-foot-high boundary fence in the process.

Judge G.A. Brickenden, who owned a line of exceptional jumping horses, was alerted to Roger's existence by a friend. Brickenden lost no time in going to see if this horse could be bought and brought into his stable, driving up to Hamburg on a Sunday afternoon.

Brickenden found Roger to be mannerly and sound of wind and limb. The farmer promised that Roger had none of the usual equine vices; his only fault was his love of jumping — a deplorable flaw, in the farmer's opinion. Trying not to appear overly eager, Judge Brickenden offered to buy Roger on the spot and take his chances with the hopping hoodlum.

The farmer would not compromise his religious beliefs by making a Sunday deal, no matter how eager he was to part company with the unsuitable equine. He refused to take payment that day, but told Brickenden to come back the following day with $250 and a horse trailer. Not surprisingly, Brickenden did.

He had got the deal of the decade. Roger moved into the Brickenden Stables and became a champion jumping horse — and the one who won the President of Mexico's special trophy. Pretty good, for a buggy horse.

Chapter 6
Big Ben: From Commoner to King

There have been thousands of good jumping horses in Canada, and hundreds of excellent ones. A few dozen were exceptional. But once in a very great while a horse comes along that is extraordinary, one that outshines all the others, the brightest star blazing in the show-jumping sky. Big Ben was such a horse.

He wasn't particularly pretty. Those in the know thought he was too big and awkward to handle the tight turns and corners of a show-jumping ring. And he made a peculiar "un-h, un-h" noise in his throat when he galloped.

A number of professional horsemen passed him up

as a jumping prospect. Then Ian Millar heard about him, saw him, tried him, bought him — and the pair started climbing the ladder to success, reaching for that elusive prize found at the upper echelons of show jumping.

The Early Years

He was born in 1976 on the farm of Jacobus van Hooydonk and Louisa van Looveren in Wuustweezel (Woost-*way*-zl), near Antwerp, Belgium. He was by the stallion Etretat (*Ate*-ra-tah), and out of the good mare Ookie (*Oo*-key). By some ever-interesting quirk of genetics, the traits of the 16 hh stallion combined with those of the 15.3 hh mare to produce a large liver chestnut colt who would grow into a 17.3 hh colossus. (By way of comparison, consider that the standard height for a door in your home is 80 inches — so if Big Ben stood in a doorway, you could only get a sheet of typing paper, lying on its long edge, between his withers and the top edge of the door. That's a *really* big horse.)

The rules of the Belgian Warmblood society dictate that, each year, all foals born of registered parents must have names starting with a particular letter. In 1976, foals' names had to start with "w." Van Hooydonk admired Winston Churchill, so he christened the gangly foal Winston.

After an uneventful colthood, van Hooydonk

turned the one-and-a-half-year-old Winston out to pasture for the summer to grow and mature. With only his younger sister and the wild birds for company, Winston ate, slept, and whiled away his "teenage" period, perfectly content to be a loner.

When he was brought in for the winter, it took an effort to get past his natural reserve and shyness. Van Hooydonk and his family used friendly persuasion — and a special treat of sugar — to curry favour with the four-legged recluse. Winston was again turned out the following spring for another season of R and R. But it was when he was reintroduced to the barn routine the next winter that he began to show his true colours.

The Unnatural Natural
Calling someone or something a freak may be a putdown in any other context, but on the Grand Prix showjumping circuit, a rider with a "freak" horse is someone to be envied. Most horses don't have a natural inclination to jump over obstacles, and those that *can* jump well have usually received hours upon hours of training. But all the training in the world means nothing if the horse doesn't have the courage, natural aptitude, and deep reserve of power required to jump huge fences again and again and again. Riders search long and hard, trying to find just such a special horse.

Like most horsemen, Jacobus van Hooydonk cared about his horses. To keep Winston from being bored, and as a suppling exercise, Jacobus began giving the horse some freedom in the indoor ring. And that's where Winston's unnatural natural traits came to light.

There was a jump set up in the ring, and Winston — under no restraint or guidance, and with no urging from anyone — started jumping it, all by himself. Jacobus was astounded: in all his years of horse breeding and raising, he had never seen anything like it. To his knowledge, Winston had never jumped anything before, and yet here he was, jumping this obstacle repeatedly, three times in a row.

When put into training under saddle, Winston proved to be as fastidious about where he placed his feet and body as he was in choosing his friends. Daniel van Hooydonk, Jacobus's son, began riding Winston in horse shows and found an eager competitor under his saddle. The horse was so enthralled with jumping that he jumped "big" — leaping much higher than the jump required, leaving lots of space between himself and the obstacle.

In the summer of 1983, Winston took first place in two of the four dressage competitions in which Daniel entered him and posted three clear rounds in four show-jumping events. Winston was now seven years old, and his life of relative obscurity was about to end.

A Rose By Any Other Name

Later in 1983, horse trainer and rider Bert Romp arrived from Tilburg, Holland, a short distance from Wuustweezel. He was in Belgium looking for likely jumper prospects, and he happened to look at the big gelding belonging to the van Hooydonks. Romp was not overly impressed with Winston's conformation, deriding his short neck, big head, and skinny appearance, but Jacobus earnestly recounted all of Winston's good qualities to Romp. When the dealing was done, Romp had purchased the tall horse for 100,000 Belgian francs (about $2000).

Romp moved Winston to his farm in Holland and put him into training. The man was exasperated by Winston's less-than-brave demeanour — the horse was a titan in size, but timorous in manner. He was afraid of many things, even something as innocuous as water. But he could certainly jump great heights.

Mrs. Romp was responsible for giving Winston the nickname by which he became famous — Big Ben — because she thought he was as tall as the London tower that houses the famous clock. Bert Romp entered Big Ben in some jumping events in Holland, but did not have stellar results. Sometimes Ben would clear the huge fences, sometimes not.

Other horsemen, on the lookout for a winner, came to Romp's farm to see Ben, but they were as unimpressed by him as Romp was. The most desirable traits for a winning jumping horse are power, speed, bravery, and manoeuvrability, like a racy sports car, and ideally, the animal should be about 16 hh.

Ben seemed to be the complete opposite of this ideal — he was more like a Mack truck than a racy sports car. Those knowledgeable horsemen, no doubt employing logic and hard-won experience in their decisions, were understandably afraid that his huge size would be a detriment to his athleticism. They concluded he wouldn't be as fast and nimble as a smaller horse. And so they all passed him by as a potential winning mount.

Crossing Paths

The people involved in Grand Prix jumping, like those in most niche sports, make up a small and close-knit society. It is not unusual for participants to know most of the other athletes competing in the sport.

Emile Hendrix rode on the Dutch national team, Ian Millar on the Canadian one. Millar admired Hendrix's ability to assess the needs of riders in relation to their riding styles (European and North American styles *do* differ), to gauge the dollar value of a particular horse on both sides of the Atlantic, and to match the best horse and rider. Millar considered Hendrix "clever, an ethical horseman, a brilliant culler of horses," and "one of the best horse dealers in the world." So when Hendrix talked, Millar listened.

Spruce Meadows, High-Flying Horse Heaven
When most people looked at the site of a former cattle feedlot outside Calgary in the early 1970s, they saw, well, a cattle feedlot. Ron and Marg Southern saw into the future and envisioned a multi-purpose horse-show facility. That vision evolved into the ultimate horse lover's heaven, Spruce Meadows, which in 2002 was ranked Number One in the world.

This Canadian crown jewel of horse complexes is home to between 80 and 100 horses all year, but that number increases to 700 or more during major events like the Spruce Meadows Masters or North American tournament. This influx of equines is housed in the 400 temporary and 300 permanent stalls.

Spruce Meadows hosts four major outdoor tournaments throughout the year, held in six different outdoor show rings, and these prestigious events — not to mention the generous prize money available — have drawn national, Olympic, European, and world champion show jumpers, all eager to strut their stuff at Spruce.

Competitions at Spruce Meadows feature some of
the finest equestrian athletes in the world.

The Spruce Meadows International Show Ring is a
picture. Jewel-green grass sets off the handsome clock-
tower entrance to the ring and the challenging jumps.
The dreaded devil's dyke is one obstacle that has
claimed many an otherwise clear round. The competitors must jump over a rail into this rectangular-shaped
corral, go down an incline to another jump over water,
then up a hill and jump back out.

With over 100 grooms, trainers, and maintenance

and administration personnel, both full-time and part-time, and over 500 volunteer workers in the summer, Spruce Meadows is a veritable beehive of activity from sun up till sun down, year round. Since the first tournament held in 1976, when approximately 12 spectators walked through the gates, this superb venue has welcomed ever-swelling crowds of show-jumping fans. The Masters Tournament held on September 8, 2002, broke all previous attendance records and posted a new high of 57,222 spectators.

It was at Spruce Meadows, in late September 1983, where Hendrix and Millar first spoke about Big Ben. Millar was headed to Belgium, and Hendrix invited him to visit while in Europe. Millar went to Brussels, completed his business, and gave Hendrix a call. The horseman, acting as an agent for Bert Romp, told Millar there was a horse he should view, stabled about an hour away from Brussels. Millar recounted this particular conversation with Hendrix, and the horse dealer's ambivalence about Big Ben, in his autobiography, *Riding High: Ian Millar's World of Show Jumping.*

"I don't know whether you'd like him or not," Millar quoted Hendrix in one chapter. "He's a great big horse. You might really hate him, and it might be a total waste of time, but there's a chance that you might find it interesting, too."

As Millar prepared to go and see the horse, he was sceptical. He concluded, logically enough, that if other expert horsemen had rejected the horse as a prospective Grand Prix contender because of his size and looks, then maybe there was something wrong with the animal. "The horse was seven years old by this time and still nobody was buying him," Millar recalled in his book. "Such a situation always makes me nervous. If my peers are saying 'no', then maybe I should listen to them.

"Everybody felt the same. They looked at this somewhat bad-tempered horse, a big monster of a thing, not the best looking, and what they really saw was the proverbial bull in a china shop. He could jump, but would he ever fit into today's indoor show rings, or handle the course? Could he be a modern-day show jumper? If he was not too clumsy, would he be able to shorten his stride? Given his size, would he be fast enough?"

However, as soon as Millar saw Big Ben, something clicked, and as a result, Millar's evaluation of the horse flew in the face of all his standard horse-buying practices. Where he normally would let a dealer present the horse to him — a process that can take over 15 minutes — Millar instead began directing Bert Romp to show him Ben's different gaits and the level of his athleticism by doing a flying lead change and trotting over a jump.

Millar said he loved Ben's trot, describing it as "loose, easy, powerful."

Everything Millar had seen about Ben thus far was pleasing to him. In another departure from normal routine, Ian asked almost immediately to ride the big horse. "For some reason I escalated the process this time," Millar explained. "Everything was telling me, 'I love this horse'."

Millar went with his instincts and made a deal for the giant horse with the attitude, paying Bert Romp $45,000 — considerably more than Bert had paid for the horse only six weeks previously. And so the big, ugly horse from Belgium with the British-sounding name made the trip to his new home in Canada, leaving his life as an equine commoner behind.

Prince in Training

Settling into the routine at Millar Brooke Farm in Perth, Ontario, Big Ben became a prince in training. As Millar started riding him regularly, he became familiar with the horse's unconventional characteristics and extraordinary abilities. He also began to figure out how to work with Ben to harness those characteristics and abilities in the show ring.

Some trainers, unable to obtain the results they desire, resort to strong-arm tactics, forcing a horse to do their will by using ever-harsher bits and training devices, but not Millar. He prefers the repetition method of horse training: whatever the lesson may be, he repeats and repeats it until the horse accepts his guidance and gets the lesson down pat.

For example, a horse must learn to shorten stride when a rider requests it. The average-sized horses favoured for Grand Prix jumping will cover 11.5 to 13 feet in a cantering stride. Course designers take this into consideration when they set up obstacles for a competition, separating them by distances that are multiples of 13-foot strides and half strides. Big Ben cantered an 18-foot stride, so he had to learn to decrease his stride length to 13 feet or less when asked by his rider.

By using his weight, posture, and leg pressure against the horse's sides, the rider causes the horse to lift his head and neck, bring his hind legs farther under him, and move into the bit. This "collects" the horse and makes him shorten his stride. To lengthen the stride (extension), the rider encourages the horse to lower his head and neck and reach his forelegs farther forward.

Big Ben was a clever horse who knew exactly what he liked to do — and what he didn't like to do. If he didn't like to do something, he tried to evade it. Although he was a talented and powerful jumper, he didn't like some of the elements of basic schooling, such as learning to adjust his stride, so he would try to avoid doing it.

Millar didn't know it at the beginning of their relationship, but Big Ben also had exceptionally keen eyesight. This sometimes caused problems. At times, Millar thought Ben was using avoidance tactics when the horse was actually noticing something a distance away that flustered him. "He was not afraid; he fears few things," Millar explained in *Riding High*. "But allowing himself to be rattled ... was his method of evasion, his way of saying, 'I don't want to be trained, I don't want to be controlled'." With patience and persistence, Millar got him to respond.

Up Like a Rocket
The making of a top-notch jumping horse is a long and exacting process. The prospective champion is brought along slowly, and a horse aged 7 to 10 years old is often considered a "young" jumper.

A horse begins in the Preliminary class, where jumps are a maximum height of four feet, and advances through increasingly difficult divisions, with the jump heights raised progressively higher in each division, before finally arriving at the most difficult level, Grand Prix, with huge hurdles set at five feet three inches. This movement through the ranks can take 5, 7, or even 10 years, and riders don't hesitate to move their mounts back down in level if the horse's performance deteriorates after the advancement. Only a small number of horses reach the top, to become consistent winners.

In contrast, Big Ben's rise to show-jumping fame was meteoric. He competed in a small jumper show in Montreal, Quebec, in the spring of 1984. He did so well, Millar moved Ben up into the Preliminary class in Edmonton, Alberta, only one week later.

The horse was also successful in Edmonton: so much so that Millar entered him in the Open Jumper division in the same show the very next day. By the end of that week, Ben took on the Grand Prix division, posting a very creditable second-place finish. One week later, he won the Spruce Meadows Grand Prix. There was no stopping him! His show-jumping career took off like a rocket.

Ben was making a name for himself, and he was gaining fans from all over Canada. "Much of the fan mail addressed to Millar Brooke Farm is not for me at all," wrote Millar, "but for a horse named Ben. Big Ben." On average, he would get 10 to 12 fan letters per week, though later, when he became sick, fans sent him get-well cards by the hundreds.

Big Ben was so popular that people frequently asked for a few hairs from his mane or tail. If everyone who asked for hair had received a strand, poor Ben would have been as bald as an egg. To accommodate fans who begged for a memento of their favourite equine star, Sandi, his groom, would paint the horse-shoe on Ben's front foot with ink and have him stand on a piece of paper, thereby signing his "autograph."

The horse was so popular that the Canadian Therapeutic Riding Association (CanTRA), which intro-duces people with physical and mental disabilities to riding as both sport and therapy, asked Ben to be their "poster horse" to help promote the group.

Tall and Short

Another amazing element in the unusual story of Big Ben is the relationship he had with his favourite groom, Sandi Patterson. Every horse has a person to whom it relates best, but the connection between Sandi and Big Ben appeared to be even stronger than normal.

Any picture of the two of them together shows a study in opposites: Sandi, the petite groom with a riot of strawberry blond locks, has the giant, dark horse stalk-ing regally along behind, reminiscent of a trim little tug-boat hauling a massive ocean liner in its wake.

At times, their relationship could be likened to that of a lowly servant (Sandi) at the beck and call of her master (Ben), dancing to his every whim. Sandi was

Ben's cleaning lady, tidying up his house — a huge box stall — every day. She was his dietician, bringing his four daily meals, which consisted of hay, hydroponically grown grass sprouts, or a specially mixed feed ration of bran, pellets, oats, molasses, and a touch of Metamucil to keep the horse's delicate digestive system chugging along properly.

The conscientious woman acted as a personal trainer, riding Ben for his daily exercise if Millar was away or otherwise unable to, and hand-walking him to keep him limber. Like a valet, she dressed him in his "clothes": saddles, bridles, protective leg boots, and blankets, keeping them clean and in good repair.

Sandi Patterson is short; her beloved charge was very tall. He had only to raise his head if he didn't want to be bridled, but because she was his greatest friend, Ben would almost always do what she asked him to do. When it was time for tacking up, he would submissively lower his head so she could bridle him.

She was Ben's personal care attendant, grooming and brushing him daily. She administered health treatments, operating an electromagnetic muscle relaxer and circulation stimulator for his back muscles. Big Ben also received laser treatments on key acupuncture points that were designed to relax other major muscles. Sandi did those treatments, too.

Sometimes she was his personal bodyguard, sleeping outside his stall in the horse-show barns, and at other times she was his appointments secretary, deciding when His Royal Highness would receive visitors and just who would be allowed to see him. With most grown-ups, he was blasé — if adult admirers came to see him in his stall at a show, he would usually pretend not to see them and turn away. But he loved children and would eagerly press his face against the bars so they could pet him.

Most of all, Sandi was his friend and companion, taking part in his antics when he was in a playful mood in the turnout paddock, or keeping him company by lying in the luxuriant green grass while he grazed nearby. While their interaction could be seen as that of a master and his servant, at other times it could only be described as a mutual admiration society, or even as an equine/human love match.

"When we first got him, Big Ben was not a people horse," explained Millar in *Riding High*. "He tolerated people because they fed him and brought him water, but he did not *like* people at all." Millar went on to recount that Patty Markell, Bobbie Donaher, Lori Green, and Sandi — the four people who looked after Ben over the years — were largely responsible for changing Ben's stand-offish behaviour.

"Does he love all people now?" Millar wrote in 1990. "No. He is not that type of horse. But, selectively, Big Ben really likes certain people, Sandi above all."

"I love him," Sandi said of her equine charge in Lawrence Scanlan's 1994 biography *Big Ben*. And the feeling, evidently, was reciprocated. "Ben will do anything for Sandi," said Millar's wife, Lynn, in Scanlan's book. "It's a matter of trust."

The King Has Quirks

No kings are completely faultless. They all have their idiosyncrasies, and Big Ben was no exception. Where other horses love apples, he detested them. His snack of choice was bran muffins, and adoring fans would send him muffins from all across the country.

He loved to play "catch the dandy brush" with Sandi Patterson and enjoyed playing the same game with young fans. He would hold the brush in his mouth, bob his head up, then open his mouth, and toss the brush to the delighted children. According to Sandi, Ben was a fine pitcher, but catching was beyond him.

More than a little like a spoiled child, Ben wanted what he wanted, and right now, please. "He's a horse with a lot of character. He thinks we are here to take care of him. He expects all the extras," Sandi told Lawrence Scanlan for *Big Ben*. "When he wants to go out, he wants to be first out and first ridden. If he's not ridden by 10 o'clock, he gets mad. He'll buck and twirl when it comes time to ride him. His electromagnetic machine has a buzzer that sounds when the time is up. When that buzzer goes, he wants off. Right away. He starts bobbing his head and pawing the ground."

Whenever Sandi had to leave Millar Brooke Farm for a few days, Ben would pout until she returned. Her return did not, however, let her off the hook. Ben would turn his back and ignore her, refusing to come to her, and grumping for days to show his displeasure at her absence.

He would not suffer even the slightest of discomforts with forbearance. Take flies, for instance. He didn't like the stable flies that would settle on his silken hide. Grant Cashmore, a New Zealander who stayed at Millar Brooke Farm for some instruction from Ian Millar, told Lawrence Scanlan about one day when he was out riding Big Ben. "All of a sudden he just stopped. There was a fly on his head. And he turned his head to look back at me, as if to say, 'Grant, would you swat that fly from my head, please?'"

Ian Millar got a hint of that sensitivity the first time he rode the horse during the pre-sale viewing. Millar used his own North American close-contact saddle; the European saddles that Ben was used to are not as flat, and they have more padding. When Millar's saddle was put on Ben, he showed his displeasure at the different feel by switching his tail and pinning back his ears with his head in the air.

"The minute I sat on him, I sensed that something was bothering him," Millar recalled in *Riding High*. "Wondering how the saddle fit, I put my finger under the front of it, only to find that it was too close to his withers. When I leaned forward the slightest bit, my weight pressed the front of the saddle down onto the wither bone ... Big Ben was *so* sensitive to this. Most horses, 99.9 percent of horses, would have tolerated this discomfort. Not Big Ben."

He would not even accept something as normal as an oral dewormer. These common paste-type concoctions kill parasites in a horse's digestive system. Ben didn't want it, and he simply raised his head so high that the grooms couldn't reach to put it in his mouth. Millar had to be cagey to combat the problem. He had Ben taken into a stable with a very low ceiling so the horse couldn't raise his head out of the way. Foiled again!

It often seemed there were no grey areas with this big horse, there was only black or white; he either liked something or he didn't. He *detested* green garbage bags because they might blow at him. They irked him so much that if he saw one when he was being ridden, he would buck and spin, succeeding on a couple of occasions in dumping Millar in the dirt.

Ben was definite about his creature comforts. In hot weather, he loved to have cold air blown on him with an electric fan. Weekly baths could be completed only if his rules were followed. It is common practice for grooms to secure a horse in cross-ties — fastening ropes on either side of a horse's halter with quick-release clips — before doing any kind of work on the animal. But of course, that's any *other* horse. Ben was an unusual case. If Sandi put him in cross-ties, he refused to lower his head so it could be bathed. His head would only come down when Sandi had removed the offending ropes.

Triple Threat

Big Ben could jump like a cat. Also like a cat, he seemed to have multiple lives, cheating death on three different occasions.

The digestive system of a horse is a delicate mechanism. When a horse has eaten too much — perhaps by overindulging on windfall apples, or after breaking into the feed bin and gorging himself — he cannot vomit. Whatever goes into the stomach must pass through the intestines and colon and be expelled as manure. If for some reason it *can't* pass through and forms a blockage, the result is a condition dreaded by all horse owners:

colic. Colic is one of the main causes of death in horses. The pain of colic is so intense that a horse will often throw himself to the stall floor and roll back and forth, trying to relieve the pain. The danger of this action is that the violent rolling can cause a twist in the bowels, which cuts off the blood supply to a section of the intestine. Without its steady supply of oxygen-rich blood, the affected part of the intestine will begin to die. If the condition is left untreated, the horse will likely die, too.

Big Ben may have been a superhorse in many ways, but he was no more immune to colic than any other equine. In March 1990, the Millar horses were in Florida for a competition. They were staying at a stable in Tampa. The sun was spilling through the trees on a warm, bright day, but a dark shadow was cast inside the barn. Ben began exhibiting signs of colic, pawing the ground and walking around and around in his stall.

Attending veterinarian Dr. Rick Mitchell told Ian that the problem was an impaction. He began treating the distressed Ben with intravenous fluids and anti-inflammatory drugs, hoping the impaction would pass. The treatment seemed to be working, but all anyone could do was watch and wait. Sandi kept Ben company; it helped to pass the time.

Suddenly, around suppertime, the mighty horse thudded to the stall floor, like a massive oak felled by the woodsman's axe, and began to thrash back and forth. In spite of her fright and the danger from his flailing hooves, Sandi dashed in to try to get Ben up and walking. Stopping a horse from rolling and keeping him walking often help to get things moving along inside.

Getting a colicky horse up is difficult. You may have to tug and pull at him because he hurts, and he doesn't *want* to get up. In some cases where the horse is very stubborn or reluctant, attendants may have to swat him with a broom, or bang a stick on a metal bucket to frighten him. However she managed it, Sandi got Ben to his feet.

She was walking Ben in the arena when Dr. Mitchell and Millar charged back into the barn. They decided to take the horse to the clinic in Ocala, Florida, about one and a half hours away, posthaste. Dr. Don Sloan advised immediate surgery; however, Millar wanted to wait just a little longer to see if the situation would possibly resolve itself. It did not. By 6:30 the next morning, Dr. Sloan was preparing to take Ben to surgery.

Colic surgery is tough on a horse. On average, the survival rate for a less severe colic surgery is 85 percent. Horses that need to have a portion of their small intestine removed face only a 65 percent chance of surviving. Most horses take months to recover, and few ever compete successfully again following their convalescence.

Dr. Sloan began the surgery and found where the blockage was. He got it to move by injecting it with saline. Luckily, he was able to avoid cutting into Ben's intestine. He advised the Millars of possible complications from colic surgery and told them, "You're not even close to being out of the woods yet. Not for six weeks, anyway." Sloan prescribed a detailed plan for Ben's recovery: constant light exercise for weeks, being led at a walk every day.

Ben recuperated far more quickly than the clinic staff anticipated. They were amazed and credited his quick convalescence to his high level of conditioning. Approximately 12 weeks after his surgery, Big Ben won the Grand Prix at the Spruce Meadows National. He was back — and as good as ever. But the shadow returned.

In the early hours of a cold January morning in 1991, Sandi Patterson found Ben walking his stall, stopping now and again to paw at the ground. His morning ration lay uneaten — never a good sign. Her heart dropped to her toes as she faced the possibility that the great horse was again colicking. She quickly summoned the husband-and-wife veterinarian team of John Atack and Linda Berthiaume, who have an equine clinic right on Millar Brooke Farm.

Ian and Lynn Millar were in New York on a horse-buying foray, 10 hours away. Sandi was finally able to contact them mid-morning to give them the sombre news. Millar spoke with Dr. Atack, who assured him everything that could be done was being done. "If he doesn't improve soon, Ian," Atack said, "we'll take him to the clinic at the University of Guelph." (Atack was referring to the Ontario Veterinary College clinic, which is at the university.)

For 90 minutes, Atack bombarded the blockage with all the standard treatments: oils, fluids, and walking. None of them worked. After tranquillizing Big Ben and giving him a painkiller, Atack had the horse loaded into a van for the six-and-a-half-hour trip to Guelph. Sandi was at Ben's side in the trailer, offering comfort and support.

It was early evening by the time they pulled into the clinic's admitting area. They had had to stop about 30 kilometres out so that Atack could give Ben another needle to ease his terrible pain.

Dr. Ron Trout was the surgeon on call that night. He assessed Big Ben's condition: high heart rate (which indicates pain), bloated belly, and a seriously swollen large intestine. All symptoms indicated that immediate surgery was imperative.

The big gelding was taken directly to the pre-op, where he was prepped and given anesthetic. Almost instantaneously, he slumped to the floor, which is in fact an operating table that is raised and lowered by hydraulics. Technicians shaved his belly and a patch on his neck, and then, to reduce the possibility of infection from contamination, they wrapped his hooves with plastic covers before draping green surgical sheets over his body and wheeling him into surgery.

Sandi viewed the whole operation on a TV monitor and watched as Dr. Trout found the blockage in Ben's grossly swollen intestine. As the vet had done during Ben's previous colic surgery, Trout injected a salt solution into the blockage. This made it wetter and allowed the vet to massage and thin it out. "Then he stopped," wrote Lawrence Scanlan in *Big Ben*, "confident that nature — Big Ben's own horse plumbing — would move it all out later. Had the surgeon been forced to remove the blockage by cutting into the intestine, the odds of recovery would have declined, for the chance of infection would have risen."

Big Ben had already beaten the odds by surviving not one, but two colic surgeries in less than a year. That was astounding in and of itself, but horses who survive colic surgery rarely, if ever, return to the same level of proficiency they were at prior to the operation. It is even more unlikely the older the horse is. Ben was now 15 years old. Was his career over?

Happily, it wasn't. Later that year, Ben won the

du Maurier International, the richest event at Spruce Meadows, for the second time and also helped Canada win the Nations Cup at the Royal Winter Fair. It looked like he could go on competing and winning forever.

But his trials were not yet over.

Highway of Horror
When Millar Brooke Farm horses commute to shows in North America, they travel in sleek silver-grey and blue horse trailers, pulled by semi-trucks. Horses face some exhaustingly long road trips because Air Canada deemed horse air transport within Canada unprofitable and discontinued it.

It was nearing midnight on May 24, 1992, and Big Ben was ensconced in his favourite stall, behind the driver's seat, as he had been on many a trip before. The gelding dozed as the rig conveyed him and seven equine compatriots through the Saskatchewan countryside on a rainy night. Their destination: Edmonton, a 57-hour trip from home. It was only the first stop on the competition trail. From there it was on to Calgary for a week-long tournament before heading back home to Ontario.

Sandi Patterson was in the passenger seat of the truck cab, her shoes off so she was more comfortable. She drifted in and out of sleep, while Ken Armstrong was at the wheel. They were in the lead, with other grooms following in passenger vehicles, and behind them, two more horse transports.

Suddenly, a vehicle going the opposite direction sped out of the night towards them. The pair in the truck cab saw with horror that it was in their lane — they were on a collision course! Armstrong made a valiant effort to avoid the vehicle, but the metal missile, travelling at 100 kilometres per hour, smashed into the front axle of the truck and burst into flames.

Without its axle, the mangled horse van became a lumbering elephant, out of control. Down the highway it slid, sideways, then headed for the ditch, where it teetered onto its right side in slow motion.

Neither Patterson nor Armstrong was seriously hurt, but Armstrong was unable to get out: his legs were pinned. Since the passenger door was jammed into the dirt, Sandi had to get out the driver's side door, which she had to reach by crawling over Armstrong.

Opening the door was a challenge. Sandi had to push it upwards, like opening the trapdoor into an attic. Truck doors are extremely heavy, and it was all she could do to hold the door open long enough for her to squeeze out of the crippled vehicle.

She sprinted down the length of the trailer, her bare feet splashing in puddles and in danger of being slashed to pieces by broken glass from the accident. She scaled the side of the toppled van to find the loading door, then struggled to get it open and look inside the trailer.

Blessedly, the lights inside the horse trailer were still working, and Sandi could see the terror-stricken horses struggling to stand upright. Since the side of the transport was now the floor, their legs flailed about, trying to gain a purchase on metal walls with their metal-shod feet. Uppermost in Sandi's mind was the need to get Ben and the other horses out. But the accident had jammed the back door shut.

Two Millar Brooke grooms who had been driving directly behind the lead truck came rushing to help. They had narrowly missed hitting both the mini-van that caused the accident and the semi-truck's front axle, which the impact had dislodged. But there was little any of them could do. They needed help, and they needed it quickly. They flagged down a passing motorist and asked him to call for fire trucks, ambulance, and police. Sandi and the other grooms tried to rescue the mini-van's driver, but the fiercely burning flames drove them back.

Meanwhile, the horses were still panicking inside the trailer. One horse had been instantly killed in the accident; another, Baarlo, had fallen under the hooves of one of the other six remaining live horses.

Within 30 minutes, ambulances, attendants, firefighters, and fire trucks began arriving to assist the victims. They released Ken Armstrong from the wreckage and took him to the hospital. It was too late for the minivan driver, who had died in the crash or the resulting fire. Now, all eyes turned to the horses.

It is not unusual for horses to survive an accident, only to bolt in panic from the scene and be struck by another passing vehicle, or go into shock afterwards and die. If there was any blessing in such a horrific collision, it was that the horses were still contained and safe from traffic. But with the back doors jammed shut, how would the rescuers get them out?

Using a crowbar — and their hands — to tear holes in the roof (now the side) of the van, Sandi and the others worked frantically to strip back a section of the roof to create a hole big enough for the horses to be brought out.

Big Ben had battered the trailer's side with his head until he poked a hole through the metal. He now sported a bad cut over his right eye. The rescuers led him out first, then they brought out the rest of the horses.

Generous and sympathetic horse owners at the Rusty Spurs Equestrian Centre made space for the original passengers of the second horse transport. Then the driver loaded Big Ben and the other injured horses and took them to the nearby Saskatoon Equine Clinic.

Besides the cut over his eye, which needed stitches, Big Ben had cuts on his legs and an abrasion on his nose. A couple of the other horses were cut by broken glass: Gusty Munroe on the knee, and Future Vision on one of his hocks. Baarlo, who initially seemed to have only minor cuts and bruises, even after he had been stood on for so long, took over a year to recover from damage to his back.

The injured horses, none of whom ultimately competed at the Edmonton show, were rested at Rusty Spurs for a week before being taken home. Being in or around trailers spooked them for months afterwards. But Big Ben was a trooper. Two weeks after the accident, he won all three classes in which he was entered at Calgary's Spruce Meadows, including a Grand Prix. It's difficult to keep a good horse down!

King of the Ring

Even after two bouts with colic and a horrifying traffic accident, Ben continued to compete successfully at the top levels. One of his favourite places was Spruce Meadows, which could have been called his second home. There he racked up more repeat wins than any other horse in history. It was the scene of some of his most impressive triumphs, perhaps because the course is ideally suited to big, ground-covering horses like Ben.

Fans by the thousands attend Spruce Meadows' big events. They sit on the grass on the viewing bank and cheer on their favourites. Big Ben and Ian Millar frequently drew the loudest cheers.

One of Big Ben's most memorable traits was his ability to go into the ring, jump every jump clean, without seeming to hurry, and yet cross the finish line, stopping the time clock, a fraction of a second faster than his closest competitors, wresting the victory from their grasp. He was a master at the timed jump-off.

So clever was he, and so fast and agile, that he could often snatch victory from seeming defeat. In the 1991 Nations Cup at Spruce Meadows, Ben approached an obstacle and soared into the air. While still airborne, but beginning his descent, he realized that the obstacle was not a single upright but a spread jump, with another set of rails in front of him. Even though his front legs had started to come down between the two fences, he was able to gather himself, tuck the legs back up, stretch out, and clear the second bar without knocking down either element. He pulled off a clean round and helped the Canadian team win the event.

The Spruce Meadows Derby is a longer course than a regular Grand Prix class: it is a real test of stamina, and clear rounds have been rare. In 1993, Ben triumphed in the Spruce Meadows Derby for an unprecedented sixth time, and for the third consecutive year.

"No other horse has come close to matching that achievement," wrote Lawrence Scanlan. "Big Ben took every jump in the derby before knocking down the very last one. This forced a jump-off against two other horses, which he narrowly won. Big Ben's record at Spruce Meadows in Calgary may never be duplicated."

In his book *Riding High*, Ian Millar said, "Two or three years at the top is all you can expect from horses competing at the grand prix level." Guess he never told Big Ben that! With over 100 wins and a total of $1.5 million in prize money garnered in a career that lasted over 11 years, Big Ben was, indeed, King of the Ring.

Last Days

In 1994, Ian Millar decided it was time for Big Ben to retire. Millar wanted his partner to bid farewell to the game while he was still at the top. The pair went on an eight-city farewell tour. Ben's fans were so eager to see him that thousands of them stood in line for several hours at each stop for a chance to say goodbye.

Ben returned to Millar Brooke Farm in Perth, Ontario, where he lived the life of luxury and ease that he so greatly deserved, with Sandi lovingly attending to his needs, as always.

In December 1999, the dark shadow of colic stole

into Ben's life for the third and final time. He had beaten the odds twice before and survived the scourge of the stable, but he was now 23 years old, an equine senior citizen. His valiant, inextinguishable spirit was growing tired, too weary to fight any longer.

When Ben developed colic on Friday evening, December 10, Dr. John Atack, his longtime veterinarian, struggled throughout the night to save him. However, in the early morning hours of December 11, Atack recommended that Big Ben be euthanized to relieve his suffering.

"He was in pain. They were at the stage of using very serious drugs to keep the pain under control," said Ian Millar in an interview in the *Ottawa Citizen* on December 12, 1999. "It was a very difficult decision."

Horse lovers around the world mourned the loss of Big Ben. The Canadian Therapeutic Riding Association (CanTRA), which received contributions in his memory, pays tribute to the gelding on its web site: "When Big Ben died in December 1999, the Canadian Therapeutic Riding Association lost a beloved friend and ambassador. He and Ian Millar were supporters of CanTRA for over 10 years, helping to raise awareness of the benefits of therapeutic riding through public appearances, a promotional video and the Big Ben Retirement Tour."

Big Ben is buried on Millar Brooke Farm, in a spot

overlooking the barns and training area. He may be gone, but he certainly isn't forgotten. As well as being a goodwill ambassador and poster horse for CanTRA, he was immortalized forever by Reeves International, a toy manufacturing company in the United States, which moulds millions of plastic horse figurines of all types and breeds.

He has been commemorated on a postage stamp by Canada Post, was made an honorary member of the RCMP Musical Ride, was inducted into the Ontario Sports Legends Hall of Fame, and, along with Northern Dancer, a famous Canadian Thoroughbred race horse, was one of only two non-human entries inducted into the Canadian Sports Hall of Fame.

Images of Ben in competition are etched forever in the memories of show-jumping fans. They can still see the tall chestnut with his head high and proud, and his tail arched. They remember how he would stride regally into the ring, his head turning and bowing from side to side like a monarch on royal parade, deigning to notice his lowly subjects. The "un-h, un-h" vocalization he made while cantering, which got louder as the competition became more intense, lingers in their ears.

This noise turned out to be not a breathing problem at all, as was assumed by so many of the prospective buyers who passed up the gelding. Instead, it was another individual quirk. It may be fanciful, but to some, Ben's chuffing noise appeared to be a self-motivational tool, his own version of the Little Engine That Could's "I know I can, I know I can ..."

Big Ben, the tall and gangly chestnut gelding from Belgium, the gelding nobody wanted, successfully made the transition from commoner to show-ring king, transformed by the patience and skill of Ian Millar, just as an unremarkable lump of carbon is transformed into a priceless diamond by the skill of a diamond cutter. He will live on in the hearts and minds of those who loved him.

Reign forever, Big Ben!

Glossary

Appaloosa: A horse breed characterized by its colourful spotted coat. Originally bred by the Nez Perce Indians in their lands around the Palouse River in the Pacific Northwest, the Appaloosa has five recognized coat patterns: frost, marble, snowflake, and the two most common, blanket and leopard spotted.

Bay: A brown coat colour (can range from deep reddish-brown to dark brown) with black mane, tail, and legs.

Blood horse: An old-time term used to describe a saddle horse or race horse of fine breeding, rather than a mixed-breed animal.

Bog-spavin: A soft swelling on the hock that can be caused by conformation fault, a strain from quick turning and fast stops, or deficiencies in vitamins A and D, calcium, and phosphorus.

Box stall: A large (usually 10 foot by 10 foot square), four-sided stall in which the horse is not tied and can move around freely, as opposed to a straight stall, which is narrower (approximately 5 feet by 10 feet), three sided, and in which the horse is tied.

Brush and mask (of a fox): The brush is another word for the tail; the mask is the fox's head or face.

Cavalletti: A small wooden jumping pole with X-shaped ends, which can be adjusted in height. They are used to train horses and riders beginning to learn jumping.

Chestnut: A reddish coat colour. The mane and tail are usually the same colour as the coat.

Dandy brush: A grooming brush with stiff, upstanding bristles. Used with short, sharp, flick-of-the-wrist action to remove dirt from the horse's coat.

Draw: To send hounds into woods or brush to find a fox.

Fault: A penalty assessed in jumper classes for mistakes such as knockdowns, refusals, and exceeding the time allowed to complete the course.

Godolphin Arabian: One of the three foundation sires of the Thoroughbred breed.

Hack: A horse available for hire, used in all kinds of service, or a horse worn out from overuse. Also, to ride or drive for pleasure, as opposed to working, i.e., racing, hunting, etc.

Hacking: A ride for pleasure, rather than for training the horses. A relaxing ride at a walk, trot, and/or slow canter.

Hock: The large bony joint on a horse's hind leg, connecting the upper and lower leg bones.

Knockdown: An obstacle is considered knocked down when a horse or rider, by contact, lowers any element that establishes the height of an obstacle. However, if the horse hits a bar and it jumps up in the air and falls back on the jump cups again, no faults are incurred.

Refusal: If a horse stops before a jump or ducks out to the side to keep from going over the jump, officials consider that a refusal. A refusal usually gives a horse four faults.

Two-point position: A riding position assumed in jumping, in which the rider's legs are against the horse's sides, with the posterior lifted up off the saddle, and the rider rising from his or her knees.

Warmblood: The term used to describe equines developed by crossing cold-blooded horses (the heavy draft breeds) with hot-blooded horses (Thoroughbreds, Arabians, etc.). Over the years, these crosses have produced "warmblooded" breeds like the Trakehner, Hanoverian, and Friesian.

Bibliography

Scanlan, Lawrence. *Big Ben*. Richmond Hill, ON: Scholastic Canada, 1994.

May, Zita Barbara. *Canada's International Equestrians*. Toronto: Burns and MacEachern, 1975.

Millar, Ian, and Larry Scanlan. *Riding High: Ian Millar's World of Show Jumping*. Toronto: McClelland and Stewart, 1990.

Bolte, Betty. *Jumping*. Chelsea House Publishing, 2001.
Draper, Judith. *Show Jumping Records, Facts and Champions*. Sterling Publishing Company, Incorporated, 1988.

Draper, Judith. *The Stars of Show Jumping*. Trafalgar Square, 1991.

Furth, Elizabeth. *Visions of Show Jumping*. The Lyons Press, 2000.

Martin, Ann. *Masters of Show Jumping.* Hungry Minds, Inc., 1991.

Hale, Cindy, and Sharon P. Fibelkorn. *Riding for the Blue: A Celebration of Horse Shows.* Bow Tie Press, 2003.

Acknowledgments

The author acknowledges the following sources for the quotes contained in this book: the historical book *Memory Meadows* by Grant MacEwan; the in-depth chronicle authored by Zita Barbara May, *Canada's International Equestrians*; Larry Scanlan's overview of Big Ben in his book of the same name; Ian Millar's autobiography, *Riding High: Ian Millar's World of Show Jumping*, which he co-authored with Larry Scanlan. For additional information the author referred to the following texts: *The Eyewitness Handbook for Horses* by Elwyn Harley Edwards, *Guide to Horses of the World* by Treasure Press, and *Basic Training for Horses: English and Western* by Eleanor F. Prince and Gaydell M. Collier.

Thanks also to the staff of the Stockman's Memorial Foundation of Cochrane, Alberta, who were invaluable in rooting out information when it eluded me. They were able to supply copies of articles from *Horse & Rodeo*, vol. 1, no. 2 (July 1962), and *Golden West* magazine (Summer 1977). As well, thanks to Mrs. Yogi Fell of South Granville, Prince Edward Island, a veritable fountain of horse knowledge, as well as to the members of the Canadian Model HorseNet, for their combined equine information. And, of course, to Audrey McClellan, editor extraordinaire and fellow horseman.

In addition, thanks to Alberta Equine On-Line, CBC Sports Online, Canadian Encyclopedia Online, the Canadian Therapeutic Riding Association (CanTRA), the *Chronicle of the Horse,* HickokSports.com, Horse-Canada.com, The Horse.com, the International Museum of the Horse, the Masters of Foxhounds Association of America, the Glossary of Horse Terms, Ohio State University (Bulletin 762-00 on Horse Nutrition), Sporting Origins, Spruce Meadows, and the World Olympians Education, for the information and quotes found on their web sites.

Photo Credits

Cover: Cealy Tetley; **Andrew Bradley:** page 101; **Glenbow Archives:** page 77 (NB-16-482).

About the Author

Debbie Gamble-Arsenault has been horse mad since she was a toddler; family rumour has it that "horse" was practically the first word she spoke.

Raised in a close-knit, loving family, long on children, but short on horses, she fed her passion for equines by collecting model horse figurines (a collection that now numbers over 800), reading horse stories, and begging rides on neighbourhood farm horses.

It seemed only natural that horses would be the first topic she wrote about when she began her writing career over 25 years ago. Since then, she has been published in numerous periodicals and newspapers across North America on a wide range of topics. This is her first book.

Debbie lives in Alexandra, a rural community on the outskirts of Charlottetown, Prince Edward Island, with her husband, Tim Arsenault, and two furry cat-children. Her hobbies include reading prodigiously, model horse collecting and showing, motorcycle touring and attending rallies, and having "tea and chat" with her friends.

The author is active in her church and Women's

Institute, as well as other community-service organizations. She is a charter member of the Island Writer's Association and has been a member of the Periodical Writer's Association of Canada for more than 15 years.

Debbie Gamble-Arsenault loves to hear from her readers. She may be reached at: 1320 Pownal Road; R.R.#1, (Alexandra); Charlottetown, PEI, C1A 7J6, or by e-mail at: dgamble@isn.net

AMAZING STORIES™

THE HEART OF A HORSE

Poignant Tales and Humorous Escapades

ANIMAL/HUMAN INTEREST
by Gayle Bunney

ISBN 1-55153-994-2

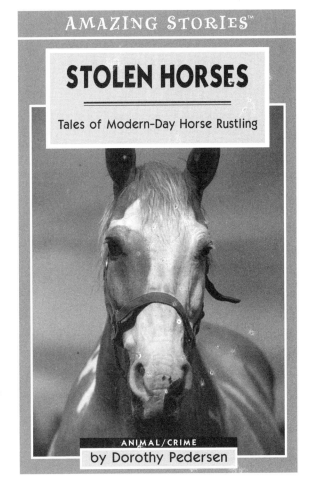

AMAZING STORIES™

STOLEN HORSES

Tales of Modern-Day Horse Rustling

ANIMAL/CRIME
by Dorothy Pedersen

ISBN 1-55153-971-3

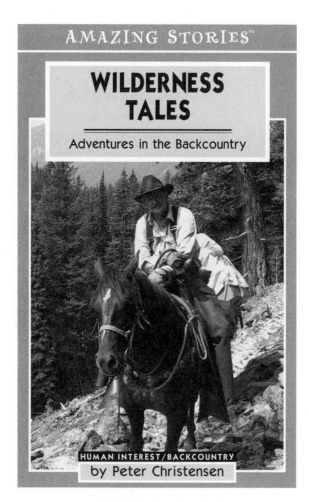

AMAZING STORIES™

WILDERNESS TALES

Adventures in the Backcountry

HUMAN INTEREST/BACKCOUNTRY
by Peter Christensen

ISBN 1-55153-987-X

AMAZING STORIES™

GREAT DOG STORIES

Inspirational Tales About
Exceptional Dogs

ANIMAL/HUMAN INTEREST
by Roxanne Willems Snopek

ISBN 1-55153-946-2

OTHER AMAZING STORIES

These titles are available wherever you buy books. If you have trouble finding the book you want, call the Altitude order desk at 1-800-957-6888, e-mail your request to: orderdesk@altitudepublishing.com or visit our Web site at www.amazingstories.ca

New AMAZING STORIES titles are published every month. If you would like more information, e-mail your name and mailing address to: amazingstories@altitudepublishing.com.

Comments on other *Amazing Stories* from readers & reviewers

"Tightly written volumes filled with lots of wit and humour about famous and infamous Canadians."
Eric Shackleton, *The Globe and Mail*

"The heightened sense of drama and intrigue, combined with a good dose of human interest is what sets Amazing Stories *apart."*
Pamela Klaffke, *Calgary Herald*

"This is popular history as it should be... For this price, buy two and give one to a friend."
Terry Cook, a reader from Ottawa, on **Rebel Women**

"Glasner creates the moment of the explosion itself in graphic detail...she builds detail upon gruesome detail to create a convincingly authentic picture."
Peggy McKinnon, *The Sunday Herald,* on **The Halifax Explosion**

"It was wonderful...I found I could not put it down. I was sorry when it was completed."
Dorothy F. from Manitoba on **Marie-Anne Lagimodière**

"Stories are rich in description, and bristle with a clever, stylish realness."
Mark Weber, *Central Alberta Advisor,* on **Ghost Town Stories II**

"A compelling read. Bertin...has selected only the most intriguing tales, which she narrates with a wealth of detail."
Joyce Glasner, *New Brunswick Reader,* on **Strange Events**

"The resulting book is one readers will want to share with all the women in their lives."
Lynn Martel, *Rocky Mountain Outlook,* on **Women Explorers**

STOLEN HORSES

STOLEN HORSES

Intiguing Tales of Rustling
and Rescues

ANIMAL/CRIME

by Dorothy Pedersen

PUBLISHED BY ALTITUDE PUBLISHING CANADA LTD.
1500 Railway Avenue, Canmore, Alberta T1W 1P6
www.altitudepublishing.com
1-800-957-6888

Extreme care has been taken to ensure that all information presented in
this book is accurate and up to date. Neither the author nor the
publisher can be held responsible for any errors.

Publisher	Stephen Hutchings
Associate Publisher	Kara Turner
Series Editor	Jill Foran

We acknowledge the financial support of the Government
of Canada through the Book Publishing Industry Development
Program (BPIDP) for our publishing activities.

Altitude GreenTree Program
Altitude Publishing will plant twice as many trees as were used
in the manufacturing of this product.

National Library of Canada Cataloguing in Publication Data

Pedersen, Dorothy
Stolen horses / Dorothy Pedersen.

(Amazing stories)
Includes bibliographical references.
ISBN 1-55153-971-3

1. Horse stealing--Canada--History. I. Title. II. Series: Amazing stories
(Canmore, Alta.)

HV6665.C3P43 2003   364.16'2   C2003-906767-X

An application for the trademark for Amazing Stories™
has been made and the registered trademark is pending.

Printed and bound in Canada by Friesens
4 6 8 9 7 5 3

For Lambros, the *only* person who cared
to learn the truth, never abandoned me,
and gave a damn if I lived or died.

Contents

Prologue

It was 4:00 a.m. on October 28, 1915, and Saskatchewan farmer O.J. Mack rolled out of bed to begin the day's chores. Heading outside, Mack struggled to adjust his eyes to the darkness of early morning. As he squinted in the dimness, he noticed that his two horses were gone. At first he assumed his neighbours had let the horses out to pasture, but as daylight broke, he realized this wasn't the case. There, on the ground before him, were the very clear tracks of two horses and one human. Mack was certain the hoofprints belonged to his horses; he recognized one set as the uncertain step of his mare. She was blind.

With mounting anxiety, Mack followed his horses' hoofprints until they ended and a set of buggy tracks started. He followed the buggy tracks for the rest of the day before finally losing them. Distraught, he then returned to his farmhouse and reported his missing animals to the authorities. But what if the authorities couldn't get the horses back? What would he do then? Mack relied heavily on his strong, working horses for the proper functioning of his farm. Without them, the farm would be in trouble.

Stolen Horses

Days passed, and Mack heard nothing from the authorities. He began to fear that his horses would not be found alive and well. This fear only intensified when the Royal North-West Mounted Police finally contacted him. The news wasn't good. They needed him to come to headquarters to identify two horses that had been discovered lying dead in a coulee.

With sunken spirits, Mack steeled himself to look at the horse heads and other body parts that the staff sergeant had brought back with him from the scene. When Mack opened a box containing the severed, decomposing head of a stolen gelding, a wave of relief engulfed him. "That's not my horse," he said, exhaling slowly. Suddenly Mack felt a renewed sense of hope. Perhaps his horses would be found after all. Perhaps his farm could be saved, and the animals would be returned safely in the near future.

Then he opened the box containing the second head, and his heart sank. "That's my mare."

Chapter 1
Cross-Border Thefts

hroughout the 1800s, it was a known fact that the quality of Canada's livestock was much higher than that of the United States'. Unfortunately, this meant that Canadian horses were frequently stolen, taken across the border into the U.S., and sold to American aristocrats for top dollar.

In New York State, horse stealing and smuggling was a lucrative job for many scoundrels. In fact, by 1812, as Canadians and Americans became entrenched in war, stealing from frustrated farmers got to be so profitable in New York that some thieves had no other form of employment. Among the most ruthless of the horse thieves at that time were the leaders of the notorious Loomis Gang.

Stolen Horses

George Washington Loomis, father of the Loomis Gang, settled in Oneida County, New York, in 1802. Though he had reportedly been chased out of Vermont for horse stealing, George was nevertheless regarded as an educated, industrious, and respected farmer. The best livestock in the county belonged to him, and his fine horses were the envy of all. At the Oneida County family home, George and his wife raised 10 children — six sons and four daughters — and each of them seemed relatively bright and likeable. The entire family treated anyone who entered the Loomis home as a welcome guest.

But the six Loomis boys were far from the charming little things they pretended to be. They were troublemakers by nature, and, undoubtedly influenced by their own father's propensity for horse stealing, they soon matured into counterfeiters, liars, and thieves.

The oldest of the Loomis sons was William. Not the brightest of the brothers, he had a disagreeable disposition and was more a follower than a leader. The second oldest son, however, was a born leader. Described as unusually bright by a former schoolmaster, Washington "Wash" Loomis was keen, perceptive, and charismatic. His way with words enabled him to disarm enemies and convince potentially damaging witnesses to lie to authorities.

Grove Loomis, third oldest among the Loomis boys, lacked the verbal abilities of his older brother Wash. Grove was a fierce man, feared by everyone. The dubious owner of several purebred horses, he was an excellent horseman, capable of riding long distances over rough terrain. His brother Wheeler, fourth in line, was perhaps the worst scoundrel of the gang. The only family member who actually served time in the penitentiary, he was said to have "not a redeeming quality." Wheeler was the gang's official scout, and therefore directly responsible for many a stolen Canadian horse being led across the border.

The two youngest Loomis sons, Denio and Plumb, were unscrupulous, but lacked the artistry, imagination, and courage of their older brothers. Neither was trustworthy, and they were quick to abandon other gang members when things got tough. Though the brothers made up the core of the Loomis Gang, many other scoundrels joined forces with the group as well.

The Loomis Gang conducted business with the utmost efficiency. Usually working under cover of darkness, they would sneak across the border into Canada and go about their thieving. Everyone in the gang knew exactly where they were going, which farms to hit, and which horses they were after. Nighttime only lasted so long, and gang members couldn't waste time getting lost on trails or chasing down a broken old nag that would only fetch the going rate for horses. Every moment's delay increased the chance that a horse's rightful owner would wake up and rush out to defend his property.

In order to reduce the possibility of getting caught, gang

members tied pieces of burlap around the stolen horses' hooves to muffle the sound of their feet hitting the ground. Once the thieves gathered up the 60 to 70 horses they came to Canada to collect, they quickly made their way to Brockville, Ontario, and then back across the border, herding their investment all the way. During the summer months, flat-bottomed boats carried the bewildered horses across the St. Lawrence River.

When safely back on U.S. soil, the gang ushered the horses over flat land to Hammond, New York, and then on to the sparsely settled town of Rossie. By the time the horses arrived in the Rossie area, they were more than ready to rest in one of the town's many hiding places.

Early on in their criminal careers, the Loomis Gang chose the tiny town of Rossie as a main hideout and terminal for their stolen horses. Located in New York's St. Lawrence County, on the southern side of the St. Lawrence River, Rossie was an ideal location for a quick nip across the border to acquire some Canadian loot — namely healthy, strong, well-fed horses. The gang liked the fact that there wasn't much in the way of open terrain around Rossie. The area, with its dense overgrowth, many rocks, and muddy footing, was the perfect place for a bunch of horse thieves and their new-found horses to keep out of sight.

But the gang liked more than just the town's location and terrain. They also liked the fact that the impoverished townspeople were too busy trying to earn a living to bother reporting suspicious activity in the area. Life was tough in Rossie. People worked hard, but their standard of living remained far below that of the southern states. Most of the residents figured their lives were hard enough without inviting trouble by ratting on a bunch of horse thieves. And, those who might have felt the urge to talk to the local constabulary were usually paid for their silence.

Every once in a while, an honest, God-fearing resident would feel inclined to act on his conscience and report the gang's activities. But these residents would quickly learn that there was worse to fear than the wrath of God. Indeed, the Loomis Gang were better friends than enemies, and anyone who was fool enough to take them on would quickly find his house burned to the ground, his livestock stolen, his character assassinated, or some such similar catastrophe.

With the Loomis Gang's growing interest in the region, it didn't take long for Rossie to become the hub of horse thievery. As former Rossie historian, the late Virgie B. Simmons, once explained, "An early hotel keeper in the village said on many a dark night he heard the thud of horse's feet passing through the dust of the crooked road to Hammond. Once he counted sixty-five of them. I doubt if that number could be found in the whole town today."

The gang had several terminals throughout New York and other states in order to facilitate the distribution of their stolen horses. Their main terminal was a property in Rossie that they rented from a local farmer named Rastus Reynolds.

They soon rigged the farm with hiding places, trap doors, and secret escape hatches. Though Reynolds later realized that his property was being rented for ill use, the gold coins handed over to him persuaded the strapped farmer that horses were a much more profitable crop than corn.

The Reynolds farm was a desirable hideout for the Loomis Gang because the property had two hidden ways to get in and out. One was located at the southern end of the Indian River Bridge and the other was located just a few yards beyond. These access points led to secret trails that wound through rocky, untracked wilderness. The unknown trails were important to the gang for the expeditious and furtive movement of the horses.

The gang couldn't let the horses rest for long in Rossie. As soon as the animals were watered and deemed rested enough, they were back on the move. Gang members, always on the alert, barely had time to catch their own breath before they were herding the animals on trails that led from northerly points to the central part of New York. Many early homes, built well back from the roads, served as beacons for the gang. A light in a particular window of a select house along the "underground horse railroad" indicated it was safe for the gang to proceed. If there was no light shining, the gang took the horses to the nearest hideout and waited. Sometimes they holed up at prearranged safe houses or hid in forests for days at a time.

Though the Loomis brothers and the rest of the gang

needed to get the stolen horses out of their possession as quickly as possible, they were careful not to rush and get caught. They were also careful not to push the animals. Under Grove Loomis's direction, the thieves knew they couldn't run the animals too quickly or recklessly. The animals were a stolen investment, and if they died en route or arrived at the point of sale looking run-down and bearing cuts and injuries, then the investment would depreciate considerably. Gang members were knowledgeable horsemen and knew how to keep the animals in good flesh.

They also knew how to alter the appearance of various horses so that it was difficult for owners to recognize their own animals — even when they'd only lost them the night before. One team of horses was bought back by its original owner, who was unaware that he was purchasing his own stolen team! The gang used dyes, silver nitrate, and other chemicals to change the look of the vulnerable animals. Sometimes a hot baked potato was bound tightly to a horse's forehead to destroy the pigment of the hair, giving the horse the appearance of having a white star on its face. Such camouflage made it difficult to identify horses and consequently prove they had been stolen. Still, whether provable or not, everyone in northern New York knew what was going on.

The hidden trails the gang used ended at Utica, New York, the location of the closest railway to the southern states. If all went well, it usually took the gang three or four days to get to Utica, where the unsuspecting horses were loaded onto trains and shipped to wealthy buyers in the South.

Throughout much of the 1800s, the Loomis Gang dominated the horse-theft industry, growing rich off countless Canadian horses, as well as animals from other states. By 1813, authorities in Canada were making an effort to do something about these thefts. That year, Colonel Frazier and his company of British Regulars were sent to the United States to look for horse thieves. When they arrived in Rossie, they quickly surrounded the town's population of fewer than 500 people. Frazier vowed to put an end to the thievery. He then left his horse and some of his men at the Rossie Hotel, and went off with a small party to search for scoundrels. By morning, his horse had disappeared. While villagers rocked with laughter, troops scurried back to Canada. Up against the cunning Loomis brothers, the Regulars were completely out of their league!

Authorities were no match for the Loomis Gang. Although the brothers and other gang members were often arrested (for thievery, plundering, hiding a fugitive from lawmen, or any other number of offences), they were rarely convicted. No sooner were gang members placed in jail than a respectable person from the community would come to sign a bond to bail them out.

As the years passed, the gang's criminal ventures blossomed into a large-scale business due mostly to wealthy Southerners who bought the horses for high prices. The biggest market and most outrageous prices in the South were to be had during the Civil War (1861 to 1865), when the Confederate army desperately needed good artillery and cavalry horses, and paid handsomely for the stolen animals.

This pressing need for horses resulted not only in a booming business for the Loomis Gang, it also created a new career track for deserters from both the Union and Confederate armies. Men adopted horse stealing with the gusto of a businessman on an upwardly mobile career path. Even Canadians joined in the theft and re-sale market to the South.

As the market grew, gang members began to notice the growing competition they were facing. It took little effort for gang members to convince many of the deserters and renegades to join their ranks and form a syndicate, ingeniously removing the competition while increasing their market share. Thieves continued to sneak into Canada and steal the best horses on the northern side of the St. Lawrence, leaving frustrated Canadian farmers struggling to find replacement animals with which to bring in their crops or provide transportation.

Every once in a while, the Loomis Gang would head to Canada to sell a horse instead of steal one. On one occasion, a Canadian buyer even made money off the notorious gang! This unusual episode began when a new neighbour of the Loomis' called on them, as was the custom back then. After introducing himself to Wash Loomis, the neighbour explained that he was a man of little means, and that he hoped he could make his way through life without neighbour troubles. Wash, playing the role of country gentleman, assured the man that he, too, hoped to co-exist, and was even willing to look out for his neighbour's interests.

Not long after his conversation with Wash, the neighbour lost his best horse. A brave individual, he walked straight to the Loomis house and confronted Wash, reminding him of his promise. Wash denied any knowledge of the missing horse and, like a good neighbour, swore he would keep his eyes open for the animal.

Unbeknownst to Wash, some of the gang had, in fact, stolen the animal, taken him across the border to Canada, and sold him. When Wash discovered this was the case, he tracked the horse down and, even though it cost him a whopping $300 to do so, returned the horse to its rightful owner. After this, Wash and his neighbour had the utmost respect for each other's strength of character, and there were no more "incidents" between them.

Grove Loomis, however, had more difficulty staying out of trouble. In 1865, Grove offered to pay a local farmer $30 for a horse, but claimed he would have to take the animal to the next train station in order to get the money. When Grove returned, he nonchalantly informed the man that he was without horse or money. After many years of silently enduring the gang's exploits, this treachery was the last straw for local farmers and the gang's other victims.

On October 29, 1865, at the height of the family's

"career," Wash Loomis was duped into getting out of bed and leaving the house to respond to a man's whispered plea to come outside and speak to him. Upon stepping out the front door, Wash was promptly attacked by an angry mob of locals, his face beaten beyond recognition, his skull fractured. As he lay dying, the small mob, consisting of three men (including the local constable), went into the house in search of Grove. There were 14 other people asleep in the Loomis mansion at the time.

The constable stood outside Grove's bedroom door and told him that he had come for him. Believing that he was being arrested, Grove got out of bed and compliantly accompanied the constable downstairs, where he was beaten to a pulp. As he screamed, his attackers covered him with kerosene-soaked sacks and blankets and set him on fire. Despite suffering serious injuries Grove lived through the ordeal, thanks in large part to one of his sisters, who threw a coat over him to extinguish the flames.

Though Grove survived, the Loomis family spirit was broken, and the gang's activities ground to a halt. Grove retired to a small farm and died in 1877. As the years went by, the other brothers retired to the farming life and passed away one by one. Wheeler Loomis, the brother who spent most of his time living and scouting horses in Canada, died at Alexandria, Ontario, on March 20, 1911. His body was returned to the United States for burial, at which time Canadian horse-owners undoubtedly breathed easier.

Chapter 2
The British Remount

On September 15, 1906, a man named E.C. Johnson spotted his stolen horse at the Calgary stockyards. The animal was standing with 115 British remounts, all headed for Montreal on the first leg of a voyage to South Africa. Johnson, eager to have his horse back, notified Superintendent R. Burton Dean of the Royal North-West Mounted Police (RNWMP) about the animal. But in the time it took Deane to confirm Johnson's claim, the horse in question had been loaded onto an eastbound train with the other remounts.

Recognizing the need for swift action, Deane immediately instructed one of his sergeants to find out who had sold the horse to the British government, but to "make [the] enquiries secretly so as not to give the thief warning." He then notified RNWMP Commissioner A.B. Perry about the situation. Before the sun set that night, Perry issued a telegram to Staff Sergeant M.V. Gallivan in Winnipeg: "One of the British remounts is alleged to have been stolen from E.C. Johnson, Calgary." Following a description of the animal, the telegram closed with, "If horse found answering this description detain it."

The train carrying the remounts was scheduled to stop at Winnipeg for refuelling, and when it did, Gallivan was standing on the railway platform, waiting to inspect the animals. He promptly found the horse and seized it on authority of Commissioner Perry's order.

Meanwhile, back in Calgary, Superintendent Deane had tracked down the horse trader who had sold the horse to the British government. The trader, George Hoadley, told Deane that he had purchased the horse the previous spring from a man named Charles MacDonald. Hoadley also acknowledged that the brands on his horse and those on the allegedly stolen horse were identical. But he insisted that the horse he had sold had been troublesome to ride, while Johnson claimed that his horse had been gentle. This appeared to be the only discrepancy between the horses. Hoadley, concerned at being implicated in horse theft, invited Johnson to talk with him — presumably to convince him that the purchase of the horse had been legal.

Two days after spotting his stolen horse, Johnson spoke

with Hoadley on the telephone at the RNWMP station in Calgary. By the time Johnson hung up the phone, he was convinced that Hoadley had, in fact, owned the horse legally, and he dropped his claim. A police sergeant also confirmed Hoadley's lawful ownership and deciphered that MacDonald had branded all his horses in the same manner. Two of these horses, which he had sold to two different buyers (Johnson and Hoadley), had been similar in appearance. The matter, it seemed, was settled.

Upon hearing this latest development, Superintendent Deane sent word to Commissioner Perry, asking him to arrange for "disposal of horse." But the commissioner could not comply; his authority was limited to sending the animal back to its owner. Suddenly, telegrams were flying back and forth as the RNWMP and other officials tried to arrange for the horse to rejoin the remounts. One of these telegrams indicated that the other 115 remounts had left Winnipeg bound for Montreal the same day that the complaint had been filed. It would be impossible to send the horse on by itself. Upon hearing this news, Commissioner Perry grew concerned. "This matter will justly cause much complaint," he predicted. He had no idea just how right he was.

Now the RNWMP had to figure out what to do with the horse they had seized. Wanting to solve the problem as quickly as possible, Superintendent Deane asked Johnson if he would take ownership of horse, seeing as it resembled his missing horse so closely. But Johnson conceded ownership to

Hoadley. Evidently he didn't want just any old horse, he wanted his own horse. Disappointed, Deane notified the commissioner: "British Government is admittedly now the owner."

The British army agent who had purchased the horse from Hoadley got involved. Unfavourably impressed, and afraid that his purchase might reflect badly on him, the agent began demanding that the RNWMP — or somebody — pay the expenses incurred for the army's loss of the horse. He demanded a lot of things, including payment for the vacant stall on the ship that had just left Montreal. Superintendent Deane complained to Commissioner Perry, "it is not easy to get him to talk reasonably on the subject." Then he restated the commissioner's fears. "No doubt the matter will be the subject of considerable complaint, but the police could surely have done nothing else than they did."

The British army did not agree. When British Colonel Charles H. Bridge, Inspector of Remounts, learned of the seized horse on September 21, 1906, he was livid. He immediately wired the commissioner: "I am now writing and demanding a refund of the sum paid for the horse. Of course the horse will now be of no use to the Imperial Government, even should the allegation of theft prove unfounded...You may however think it right to enquire into the circumstances attending the seizure of a horse merely alleged to be stolen."

Apparently, Colonel Bridge thought the allegedly stolen horse should have been allowed to continue the journey to Montreal and board the steamer bound for South Africa. But the RNWMP knew they would have come under severe criticism if they had permitted such a thing and then found out that the horse had indeed been stolen.

In such an event, would Colonel Bridge, or anyone else for that matter, have taken the animal out of service and returned it, by ship from South Africa, to its rightful owner? In such circumstances, the British army may have been considered party to the theft. But Bridge regarded the police seizure of the horse as akin to theft from the government, and the tone of his letter signalled what was to come.

As the RNWMP and British army tossed the horse's fate back and forth, it became abundantly clear how the mounties earned their respected reputation around the world. Those early lawmen were truly dedicated. They took great pride in doing the right thing, and were prepared to make the necessary effort to bring it to pass.

Throughout his communications with the police, Colonel Bridge's chief complaint seemed to be that he had not been personally notified of the seizure, but had found out about it five days after the fact from a foreman.

As the mess got murkier, the Secretary of the Territorial Live Stock Association C.W. Peterson, got into the fray. He was required to look after the horse until the fate of the animal was determined. A rather forceful fellow, it took all the RNWMP's patience and devotion to duty to communicate politely with him. He referred to the RNWMP as simply the NWM Police, disregarding the honour bestowed on the force in 1904 by King Edward VII, when, in recognition of service to the Crown, the law enforcement agency was given the "Royal" prefix. "The horse is now on our hands as a result of this idiotic blunder," Peterson wrote. He vehemently demanded that legal action be taken against the original complainant, Johnson.

But Johnson couldn't be faulted. There was no evidence of malicious intent on his part, nor did it seem that he had made the claim of theft recklessly. The horses had been almost identical, and an honest mistake had been made.

By September 24, the Department of Militia and Defence in Ottawa had received a letter from Bridge, which described the seizure of the horse and accused the RNWMP of being "high-handed." Wanting to address this matter quickly, the department contacted Lieutenant Colonel Fred White, Comptroller for the RNWMP, to make him aware of the letter. "No doubt the seizure of the horse was all correct," White was told, "but it would seem that immediate notice ought to have been sent to its then owner, especially as he was a Government official purchasing for the British Government. It occurred to [the department] that perhaps you ought to know of this."

As early as September 26, Lawrence Fortescue, filling in for Fred White, sent a handwritten note to Commissioner Perry in Regina suggesting that the best plan would be for the police to take ownership of the horse, purchasing it from the "Imperial Army."

He then requested that Perry give him a full report on the case. Commissioner Perry was not amused. He replied to Fortescue, "My Dear Fortescue: I have your semi-official letter … I have nothing to say in the matter."

The same day that Perry wrote to Fortescue, Colonel Bridge sent another telegraph to Ottawa. "Will accept one hundred and sixty dollars for horse. Am leaving for England and can ill spare time personal interview. No wish to dispute your opinion as to legality of seizure." Officials in Ottawa breathed a collective sigh of relief. All they had to do now was sign a cheque, and then they could finally close the file!

But remarkably, almost 100 more notes, letters, and telegrams were to pass between the police and army brass before the matter was resolved. On October 4, Lieutenant Colonel White sent a telegram to Commissioner Perry, repeating Fortescue's suggestion that the RNWMP buy the horse. This time Perry replied, "Quite willing to take over horse."

Upon receiving Perry's approval, White sent another telegram to Colonel Bridge: "If it will be a convenience to you we will take over horse held at Winnipeg, we repaying you purchase price."

It looked as though a settlement was close at hand. But for unknown reasons, it took Bridge three days to reply to White's note, and when he did so, he changed his previous offer: "Impossible to now take delivery of horse seized Winnipeg but I claim his purchase price plus all expenses."

He followed the telegram with a handwritten letter in which he complained at length about not having been notified directly about the horse's detainment. In the letter he also asked that his Canadian agents be contacted to arrange the settlement.

Not through yet, Bridge then undertook an action that conveyed his fierce determination to be reimbursed in full, to the penny: he contacted a law firm. His lawyers proceeded to write a menacing letter to the RNWMP. From the mounties' perspective, it was a dirty, underhanded thing to do under the circumstances, but they showed admirable restraint.

With a level head, Lieutenant Colonel White wrote a lengthy reply to Bridge. "It is scarcely necessary to remind you, with your knowledge and experience, that combinations for the illegal possession of horse flesh are always active, and it is only by prompt action on the part of the Police — sometimes on vague information — that horse stealing is kept in check, a condition not limited to Canada. You seem to feel injured that direct communication was not made to you of the seizure of this particular horse. Now from my point of view I think the proper person to notify you was your Agent who had charge of the animals."

White gently, but firmly, put things in perspective while maintaining a dignified stance. "I trust you will concede that the Police did all that was reasonable under the circumstances," he concluded, reminding Colonel Bridge that the RNWMP had offered to buy the horse for use in the police mounted unit, but had not received a clear response in the affirmative or otherwise.

The letter proved effective. Bridge immediately contacted his Canadian agent and told him that White was willing to buy the horse and pay his expenses, and that he approved of the offer. But, not quite able to be as affable as White, Bridge added, "unless you think matter gone too far."

Just when it looked like the horse had found a rather enviable home, Bridge had brought everything to a halt again so that his agent could decide if the matter had "gone too far." During this delay, officials from the Canadian Pacific Railway (CPR) appeared on the scene. They were holding the RNWMP responsible for horse-related costs. It is almost unbelievable that this horse could unwittingly cause so many people such a painful headache for such a long time. (One can only wonder what impact it's gentle twin had on the world at large!)

The RNWMP waited to hear from Bridge's Canadian agent. And continued to wait. Frustrated by the ridiculous delay, Superintendent Deane went into action once more. He discovered that the agent had changed employers. Deane quickly tracked him down in hopes of doing damage control. By now everyone was squirming at the bureaucratic mess that had evolved.

Deane learned that when Bridge had asked the agent to let him know if the matter had gone too far, the agent had replied with a telegram the same day. "Let Police take horse," he'd said. But the telegram had not been delivered. In fact, it had completely disappeared. Had that message been delivered, the matter would have been closed in late October. But without the telegram, one of the most frustrating horse theft investigations in the history of the RNWMP had been stalled yet again.

Once Deane tracked down Bridge's ex-agent, it was full steam ahead one more time. Commissioner Perry personally instructed Gallivan to make the best possible arrangements for the horse, as it was being acquired for use in the mounted unit.

Everyone wanted this case closed. White worked quickly, getting statements and signatures and paying bills before another wrench could be thrown into the mix. The purchase price of the horse was $160. The CPR submitted a transport requisition for $20. The RNWMP also paid out $40.05 for the horse's keep while it was detained in Winnipeg. In all, costs totalled $220.05 — almost double the normal price for a police horse.

Perry, despite complaining about someone else issuing the requisition for the animal's care, attributed the mammoth expense of the dozens of telegrams that had been exchanged to "ordinary" police expenditures.

Petty complaints and requests for signatures verifying small expenses continued to be exchanged among officials. The most blatant "dig" came from White himself, in a letter to the War Office in London, England. Detailing the expenses incurred, he stated, "It is a case of having to pay dearly for a friendly, but unappreciated, effort to assist another branch of the public service." He then promptly wrote his closing salutation: "I have the honour to be, Sir, Your obedient servant."

White sent the correspondence and then informed the clerk of the Privy Council in Ottawa that the horse had been purchased for $160. On May 1, 1907, White received a reply from the War Office in England, thanking him for payment received and stating, "I am to add that the Army Council regret the trouble and expense which have fallen upon your department in connection with this matter."

With the closing of this amazing case, one has to ponder the influence it had on the nameless horse. Although most horses come out of theft situations worse off than they went into them, this is definitely one case where the horse benefited from being thought stolen. Even if the animal had survived the gruelling journey to South Africa, the Boer War had not been long over, and it's doubtful what kind of life the animal would have had. Instead, the horse gave its life to the service of honourable men, and their admirable Force.

Chapter 3
Tracking Jack Anderson

On July 20, 1915, 27-year-old J.C. Clark gathered some camping gear and a .22 rifle, hitched his buggy to a couple of horses, and left the farm where his mother and brother were living. With several theft convictions under his belt and a string of failed jobs behind him, he was more than ready to fulfill his entrepreneurial spirit.

Clark had immigrated to Canada from England in the early 1900s. He stood about five feet, 10 inches tall, and had a mouth filled with decaying teeth. His dark brown hair, parted down the centre of his head, was allowed to grow long in the front to cover a scar on his right temple. The scar was the result of a horse's hoof making forceful contact with his head

— perhaps that was when Clark began to think differently.

The evening after he left his mother and brother, Clark halted his horses at the top of a hill near Assiniboia, Saskatchewan, and surveyed the countryside. As he took in the view, he saw eight head of horses at pasture, and among them, two Clydesdale mares with their foals. The two mares were grazing contentedly, one with a yearling filly nearby, the other with a suckling colt. Quick as a flash, Clark harnessed the two mares to a brand-new democrat buggy that was parked close by and with the two youngsters in tow, ran the horses south at a fast pace.

Tucked in the southeast corner of Saskatchewan, Assiniboia is located about 80 kilometres from the Montana border and 180 kilometres from the North Dakota border. Though tempted by his proximity to Montana, Clark knew that as soon as word got out that the Clydesdales and their foals had been stolen, authorities would be waiting for them at the nearby border. He decided to take the longer route to North Dakota, stopping along the way to visit an acquaintance named Ernest Counce, who lived near Viceroy, Saskatchewan.

By his own admission, Counce had been a lifelong crook, but he had settled at his present abode in an attempt to escape his old acquaintances and turn his life to the good. Unfortunately, Counce found that his old associates were happy to follow him, just to maintain friendly ties. When Clark arrived, he wanted something to eat, and Counce generously provided breakfast for both him and a hired hand by the name of Jack Anderson.

When breakfast was over, Clark led Counce and Anderson to the northeast side of Counce's pasture. There, standing in a coulee just beyond the property, were the four stolen horses and the democrat buggy. Clark and Anderson hid the buggy, hobbled the mares in some nearby bushes, then hogtied the foals and set about making them look older.

Soon after, Clark took the two mares to North Dakota. By crossing the border into the United States, he was immediately guilty not just of horse theft, but of smuggling as well. The closest settlement in North Dakota was Fortuna, and Clark tried to unload the horses to a resident named John Lenniger for a mere $250. Lenniger wasn't sure that he liked the look of Clark, and he asked straight out if the mares were Clark's to sell.

"I got them from my brother-in-law, William Card, of Rudser," Clark lied.

Clark had only been in Fortuna for three days when he discovered that Lenniger had sent someone to verify his information. Immediately, Clark took his leave, scuttling off with the two mares and desperately trying to sell them to anyone he encountered. He got as far as Crosby, North Dakota, where he was arrested and charged with smuggling Clydesdales into the United States.

Meanwhile, a Royal North-West Mounted Police Officer named Detective Sergeant Reames had been making inquiries about the stolen horses in Saskatchewan's Viceroy District. In early August of 1915, he was sent to Crosby, North Dakota, to ascertain whether the horses Clark had had in his possession at the time of his arrest were those belonging to Mr. Woods of Assiniboia. If they were, Reames was to ensure that extradition proceedings were commenced.

Reames made a positive identification of J.C. Clark, and then looked over the weary mares. One had a serious rope burn on her right forefoot — the result of being hobbled. "This team has evidently been travelled very fast recently and were almost done up," Reames noted. He determined that the mares closely resembled the description of Mr. Woods's horses. He laid a charge against Clark, under the North Dakota Criminal Code, for having stolen the mares in Divide County, North Dakota. Though this charge was not accurate, U.S. law allowed that horses stolen in any county, state, or country could be declared as having been stolen in the county in which the offender was arrested. As Reames later explained, "The charge … was laid merely to hold Clark on until the owner of the team could be gotten to Crosby to identify them."

News of Clark's arrest reached Counce and Anderson a week later by way of a letter sent from Clark himself. The minute Anderson read the letter, he moved into high gear. "He lit out with the two colts for Montana," claimed Counce.

Indeed, Anderson took off so quickly that Counce, left behind, didn't see the law coming for *him* through the dust.

Sure enough, Counce was arrested and remanded for 16 days, pending further investigation. Meanwhile, Clark escaped from custody in North Dakota. Without the luxury of time, he was unable to select a decent riding horse to steal, and had to settle for the first animal he came across — an old, tired horse with visible injuries to its legs and feet. Somehow, the animal got Clark to Counce's farm where, in Counce's absence, Clark holed up for a couple of days. Then, like most men on the run, Clark became nervous that the law would sneak up on him, so he moved on to his brother's farm.

By the time he got out of jail, Counce was furious. He hadn't appreciated being incarcerated, especially as he'd been trying so hard to go straight. He was still licking his wounds when Clark, carefully avoiding authorities, made his way back to Counce's house and knocked on the door. Much to Counce's annoyance, Clark hung around, hoping that Anderson would show up.

After a couple of days, Clark left, only to return a month later, still on the run. Wanting Clark out of his life for good, Counce ordered him to leave. "You're no damned good," he yelled, "you got me into trouble once and you're a black bungler!"

Clark left, but returned again a month later, still wanting very much to get in touch with Anderson. This time, he was at Counce's less than three hours when Anderson arrived with a buggy and team.

Anderson and Clark left the next day for Montana,

where they went into big-time horse stealing, having as many as six stolen horses on hand at any one time. They enlisted the services of other horse thieves, and before long, their band of criminals was enjoying a fair deal of notoriety. The group stole and sold horses throughout Montana, North Dakota, and southern Saskatchewan. They hid the horses at the farms of friends or relatives until the animals could be unloaded. And they cared not one toss about the welfare of the animals.

On October 28, 1915, Clark and Anderson went on a stealing spree. They stole three horses from a pasture near Avonlea, Saskatchewan, and then went on to take two large horses from a barn 11 kilometres to the south. The two large horses, belonging to a farmer named O.J. Mack, were stunningly flashy and handsome. When Clark and Anderson went to hide the animals near Counce's farm, Counce warned the men that they'd never be able to sell the two large horses because they were so identifiable. Unconcerned, Anderson responded, "I'll soon ditch them."

In December of 1915, Clark returned to Counce's farm on two occasions. The first time, he arrived with a couple of horses that Counce recognized as belonging to a neighbour only a few kilometres away; the next time, he turned up with a team of horses that impressed Counce so much he offered to buy them — an offer that Clark cunningly refused. The men became embroiled in an altercation over the team, and Clark left, telling Counce's wife that he couldn't stand her husband any longer.

Months later, on March 30, 1916, Anderson showed up at Counce's place while Counce was away. Mrs. Counce, however, was still at home, and it wasn't long before she and Anderson were frolicking in the hayloft. The new couple planned to ride off into the sunset together the next time Anderson left for Montana. But for now, Anderson was content to enjoy the warm days of summer at Counce's homestead.

One night, after Counce and his wife had an argument, Anderson decided to make his move. In no time, he and Mrs. Counce were headed to the Montana border, with Clark tagging along as babysitter to Counce's two children. "He stole those that were nearest and dearest to me," Counce later said of Anderson.

Around this time, the RNWMP was beginning to dedicate serious manpower to its investigation of Anderson and Clark. Still trying to leave his life of crime behind, and also wanting revenge, Counce revealed all he knew about the thieves to Staff Sergeant Mundy, who had been assigned as lead investigator on the case. Counce also filled Mundy in on the latest news about the two beautiful mares that had been stolen from O.J. Mack. "I am since informed that they are laying dead in a coulee, with bullet holes through their heads," Counce said.

When he discovered the fate of the horses, Mundy was required to gather evidence. "I got possession of the heads of the two beasts, as well as portions of the hides, where brands and scars should be, and enough of the leg to show peculiarities," he reported. He then took the heads, legs, and hide samples to Assiniboia so that they might be preserved as court evidence.

As Mundy continued to gather evidence against the thieves, Clark and Anderson set up house in Montana with Counce's little missus. When Clark's company was no longer welcome — perhaps because he'd done some furtive bungling around the house — Anderson gave him his marching orders. Then Anderson made an honest woman out of Mrs. Counce and — legally or otherwise — she became Mrs. Anderson. In no time, the Andersons were parents to two additional children.

With his large family to feed, Anderson felt the need to further expand his horse thieving business. His band snatched animals from the Glasgow area of Montana, and sold many just south of the Saskatchewan border at Scobey. As the thieving continued, the pile of stolen horse complaints on the Glasgow sheriff's desk grew higher.

Meanwhile, Mundy was still discretely sniffing around, trying to get evidence against Anderson and Clark that would hold up in court. To prevent word reaching the crooks that a policeman was making inquiries, Mundy presented himself as a livestock insurance agent to any potential witnesses. He gave the following report to his superiors:

News travels very quickly between Crooks of this kind

Tracking Jack Anderson

... if extradition is to be asked for, the applications must be
rushed through, in order that the chase may be taken up not
later than Wednesday or Thursday of this week ... one thing I
am sure of, and that is that there is no use relying upon the
officials in Valley County or Phillipps County to locate
[Anderson and Clark]. It is a question of us going over the
ground ourselves ... and if possible, taking with us a man
specially sworn in at Glasgow, to effect arrest, a man that is
not known as a deputy. To do this may entail considerable
time and expense, and will require the work of two men, with
full privilege to act as appears best to them ... Corporal
Worgan of Ogema knows Anderson and Clarke. He is a reli-
able man in a tight corner, and if I am to go on the work, I
would specially ask that he be detailed in plain clothes and
that a purely civilian outfit be supplied us. This should consist of team, and democrat, saddle horse, small tent and
camp outfit, rifles.

Inspector Denis Ryan, Mundy's superior officer, con-
curred with Mundy's recommendations. He was still sore at
U.S. law enforcement for letting Clark escape custody after
they'd nabbed him in North Dakota for the theft of the
Clydesdale horses. Ryan appealed to the commanding officer
of the Regina District of the RNWMP, noting that Clark and
Anderson were "notorious horse thieves, and a menace to the
stock-owners of this Province, I therefore beg to recommend
that no expense be spared to capture them."

Were it not for the fact that so many people were willing

to give the crooks a hiding place and warn them of police movement, the expense factor may have been much less of a police worry. But with this kind of help from civilians, Anderson and his band of thieves were becoming increasingly cocky, reckless, and dangerous. The RNWMP was eager to stop the stealing, and Mundy gave the case his undivided attention.

On September 4, 1916, Mundy found Clark and Anderson in Billings, Montana. The two thieves were involved with a man who was about to ship 150 head of horses into Canada to sell to the unwary. As Mundy continued to work incognito, almost single-handedly gathering evidence, he became concerned about whether or not fellow lawmen in the area would bungle his case. "I know of my own experience that the Deputy Sheriff at Zootman, one Riley Brooks, is a crook of the first order, the Sheriff of Phillips County is nearly as bad, and that to use either of those men on our work, would spell certain failure. They do not do their duty, that's all there is to it," he reported.

The RNWMP took Mundy's concerns to heart, and as he got closer to making an arrest, his superiors assigned him the help of another lawman, and a car — which promptly broke down three kilometres from the Montana ranch that Mundy planned to use as a home base. His new partner took the car to be repaired while Mundy headed to the ranch on foot.

The ranch was located close to Anderson's farm, and Mundy stopped for a while to stake out the thief's property.

Through his binoculars, he saw Anderson drive up to the farmhouse and go inside. When no one came out of the house, Mundy started back to the ranch, planning to have supper and return after dark to raid the Anderson property. But before he reached the ranch, he unexpectedly came across a cache of three fillies and two grown mares, one of which had a suckling foal. The mares were harnessed and hobbled; the foal was badly cut up from wire fencing, so exhausted that it lay flat out on the ground, unable to move.

Knowing time was of the essence, Mundy walked quickly on to the ranch, where he hoped to find a horse that he could use for transportation. A hired hand was there with an old mare that he'd been riding all day. She was stiff and slow, with tender feet. Hoping another horse would become available soon, Mundy decided to prepare himself some grub and wait. But before he was able to finish his supper, he spotted, through his binoculars, someone riding in the direction of the cached horses. He rushed out the door and hoisted himself onto the old mare; the other rider spotted him and immediately picked up the pace.

Mundy rode straight for the rider, and when there were about 90 metres between them, he pointed his rifle and yelled, "Stop in the name of the RNWMP!" The rider uttered something unintelligible and continued on. Both horses were going full tilt. Mundy fired a warning shot in the air and then aimed at the rider's horse. As he did so, the old mare he was riding stumbled and somersaulted, and Mundy landed hard on the parched ground. The rider continued over the hills. Mundy remounted and followed. He got within about 350 metres then jumped off the mare, took steady aim, and fired five shots. Watching them ride off into the darkness, he saw the rider's horse begin to limp.

Positive that the rider was Anderson, Mundy returned to the cached horses and waited. When no one came for the animals, he and the old mare drove them to the nearby ranch for safety. Then he returned to the Anderson property to watch the house. The night was dark, and thick fog hid the moon. Mundy waited all night, but nobody came to the property or left it.

Just as the sun began to rise, Mundy snuck up to the house and pulled a one-man raid. He found Anderson's wife inside, but she claimed to be home alone, insisting that no one but the mailman had been to the house for days. Mundy, however, didn't overlook the fact that the dinner table, which hadn't been cleared, was set for three people.

Frustrated, Mundy left Mrs. Anderson and returned to the ranch. He had no idea who owned the horses he had taken under care, but was convinced they were stolen. Afraid that Anderson would return to re-steal them — he'd been bold enough to steal horses that were court exhibits against him — Mundy sent the animals to the police pasture at Swift Current, where he knew they'd be well cared for until their owner claimed them.

While Mundy continued to stake out the Anderson

house, another 40 head of horses was stolen nearby. "People here carry on their stock raising in fear and trembling of the Anderson gang," he reported.

On October 6, 1916, Counce gave another statement to police in which he identified several of Anderson's hiding places and suggested that these were the places where Mundy might look for him. "Anderson, Clark and Sparks (a cohort of Anderson's) are always aware of the police being in the vicinity and know just what is going on at all times," said Counce. "The only way to catch Anderson is to lie in wait for him at one of these caches, or for a couple of men to wait at each cache, and get him as the other people are succouring, because he pulls out in the early hours of the morning."

Counce's information, coupled with information that Mundy had obtained from two Montana constables, set the groundwork for arrests. "I learned that Sparks had recently driven a team to death," reported Mundy. Two days after these horses were stolen just south of Swift Current, they were driven to death, dying on the banks of a creek, where they were left. "I came here with my informant and this morning went over and examined the horses, one of them a mare and the other a gelding," said Mundy. The men pulled the gelding out of the creek and found it answered the description of the stolen gelding. "If the owner identified this horse, the possession of it by Sparks here can be proven by several witnesses, we can then tie Sparks up, and that will be the key-note to the whereabouts of Anderson," explained Mundy.

Sure enough, Mundy's plan worked. On October 11, 1916, the night guard on duty in Regina received a handwritten telegram for Superintendent McGibbon of the RNWMP. The sender was Mundy, in Montana, and the message read: "[Anderson and Ed Sparks] under arrest here to-night hurry along extradition papers both temporarily held on American warrants."

Clark was not arrested; he had disappeared. But with the other arrests began a mountain of paperwork required to get the scoundrels sent back to Canada to stand trial. Adding emphasis to the importance of the extraditions, Mundy informed his superior officer that there was approximately 35 head of horses loose on Anderson's range. Mundy was holding 13 head. "Shall I have balance rounded up?" he asked.

The RNWMP took a flood of depositions from those who'd had their horses stolen, as well as from Counce and other witnesses. By then, the circumstances of many of the victims were serious. O.J. Mack was visibly impoverished. He had used his horses every day to toil his fields. His situation was so dire that a police report on his ability to attend Anderson's preliminary hearing said: "From the appearance of his farm and surroundings I would judge that he is in very poor circumstances and not at all in a position to pay his own way." Police paid for Mack's transportation to the hearing so that he could be a witness and help put Anderson in jail.

Anderson and his gang would have continued to wreak havoc on other people's lives and horses while remaining untouched by the law had it not been for the work of RNWMP Staff Sergeant Mundy, and the significant aid he received from Ernest Counce. Both settlers and horses suffered when horses were stolen, and it took the courage of men like Counce, and the bravery and competence of men like Mundy, to bring them relief through justice.

Chapter 4
Name That Crook

On October 7, 1915, a telegram was sent to the Shaunavon, Saskatchewan detachment of the Royal North-West Mounted Police. A constable was needed immediately in Scotsguard, about 24 kilometres away as the crow flies. Constable Perry set out for Scotsguard the following morning, and soon met up with the telegram's sender, a Mr. Remackell. Though Remackell himself had not been involved in any illegal conduct, he was aware of some, and had taken it upon himself to alert the police. According to Remackell, Ted Williams, an employee of the Scotsguard Livery Barn, had disclosed that he'd stolen a couple of horses and had subsequently sold them to an unsuspecting farmer by the name of Harry Bolleson.

Since then, Williams had last been seen walking in a southerly direction, away from town.

Constable Perry searched the Scotsguard area but was unable to locate Williams or anyone answering his description. However, as he gathered bits of information from several locals, he began to suspect that Williams was actually Art Smith, a thief whom authorities were already chasing. Perry returned to Shaunavon and picked up some WANTED posters that showed a picture Smith. He then returned to Scotsguard and showed the posters to the locals. Several people recognized the man in the picture as Ted Williams. Constable Perry now knew one of Smith's aliases. The WANTED poster also described the bay-coloured horse that Smith had last been seen riding. As it turned out, the horse's description matched perfectly with one of the animals sold to Bolleson.

Further investigation on Constable Perry's part revealed that Smith had arrived in Scotsguard with the two stolen horses on September 6, 1915. He had simply ridden in one day on a slim, branded, bay gelding, his hips rocking gently to the rhythm of the horse's stride. He was all dressed up in a brown and black mackinaw coat, pigskin boots, and a felt hat, and he led another horse: a smaller, grey gelding with a dark mane and tail. This horse wasn't branded, but it had a split on its left front hoof that was bad enough for people to notice.

Soon after his arrival in Scotsguard, Smith got a job at

the livery barn. Within a month, he revealed to two men who also worked there that he had stolen the bay horse from another livery barn in Harlem, Montana. He also let it be known that Mr. Bolleson had purchased the two horses for $100.

"I got these horses from a ranch down south," Smith had told Bolleson. "They've been working all summer long. They're a good pair and well worth the $100, sir."

After having looked them over, Bolleson had reached into his pocket and produced $100, for which Smith then provided a clear bill of sale. Of course, he'd signed the bill of sale "Ted Williams." Poor Bolleson. He'd lost $100 and hadn't even known that he should have been stunned.

Constable Perry knew that if Smith was crooked enough to steal horses, he was probably guilty of other crimes as well. An additional mountie, Constable J.H. Birks, was assigned to the case. Birks discovered that Smith had recently swindled another Scotsguard resident: he had sold a stolen saddle to Robert Stevenson. With the money from this sale, plus that of the horses, Smith went on a shopping spree, buying himself new pants, boots, and a cap.

After learning that Smith was still in the Scotsguard area, it wasn't long before Constable Birks tracked him down at the livery barn and arrested him. Following the arrest, Birks requested a remand, and Smith found himself confined to the guardroom in Maple Creek, Saskatchewan, for eight days while Birks gathered evidence for his trial. But when

Birks made his way across the border to gather much of this evidence, he soon learned that Smith's movements in the United States were not so easy to trace.

While he was in the U.S., Smith had done his best to conceal his activities and confuse anyone trying to follow his trail. He may not have been overly smart, but he was cunning. So cunning, in fact, that in the months leading up to his arrest, he'd managed to involve two teenagers from Shaunavon in his crime sprees on both sides of the border.

These teenagers were Bernard Madden and Perrine Hitchcock, friends whose fathers each owned homesteads in the Shaunavon area. In mid June of 1915, months before Smith's arrest, Madden and Hitchcock embarked on a trip to Harlem, Montana. Madden was in search of cattle to purchase for his dad's herd, and Hitchcock was looking for land.

Around the same time that Madden and Hitchcock were preparing for their trip south, Art Smith was making the acquaintance of a man named Charles Marsh at a Native camp near Harlem. Smith asked Marsh for a ride into Harlem, and Marsh obliged. Marsh's slender four-year-old bay horse carried both men the 20 kilometres into town. That night, the horse disappeared.

On June 16, Madden and Hitchcock rode into Harlem and put their horses in the livery barn. While there, they met the barn's newest employee: Art Smith. Hitchcock was immediately drawn to Smith. He hung around with the horse thief all evening and for most of the following day. Madden, however, had no desire to spend all his time in a livery barn; he left Hitchcock at the barn, paid a visit to the pool hall, and then went to see a movie.

When the movie ended (at about 9:00 p.m.), Madden and Hitchcock met up, as arranged, and left town. Madden rode his horse and Hitchcock walked alongside him, leading his own horse. After travelling about two kilometres, Hitchcock said, "I ain't walking any more. There's a train coming close by soon. I'm taking the train." He then took the saddle and bridle off his horse and set the animal free in a nearby pasture.

Madden couldn't help but notice that Hitchcock had found himself a pretty swanky saddle. He noticed it because his own was old and long past its prime. In fact, it was broken and thoroughly uncomfortable to ride in, but Madden and his father were unable to justify buying a new one when more cattle were needed first.

With Hitchcock gone, Madden rode on towards Willesden, North Dakota, alone. Not expecting to see anyone again before dawn, he was surprised after a couple of hours to hear the sound of hooves beating against the ground. They were moving fast and getting closer. Suddenly, out of the dark came Hitchcock, riding a buckskin horse with a brand on its left thigh. Behind him was Smith, riding a bay gelding.

"I changed my mind," Hitchcock said when he caught up to Madden. "Why pay for the train when you can ride a horse?"

"Where'd you get the horses?" asked Madden.

The two men smiled. "We got 'em."

Suspicious, Madden eyed the men and animals.

"What's the matter? You think we can't get horses when we need 'em?"

Not knowing what to say, young Madden let the subject drop.

For about a week, the trio cruised around the countryside. When they were just east of Grass Range, Montana, Hitchcock decided to trade horses with the only storekeeper in town. In exchange for the stolen gelding, Hitchcock received a bay mare. Smith also made a few trades, and the three men resumed their hobo lifestyle, riding past small towns in Montana and North Dakota, and leaving a string of theft victims in their wake.

In Beach, North Dakota, Hitchcock traded his horse again, this time for one owned by the milkman. Madden, following Hitchcock's lead, decided to trade his horse, too. He swapped animals with the mailman at Beach, ending up with a black, branded gelding with a bald face. The animal was so conspicuous that it would have been easy to pick it out in a line-up. Clearly, Madden was not cut out for a life of crime.

The men rode on to New England, North Dakota, where Hitchcock traded horses again. The bay mare he had been riding became a bay gelding — all that appeared to change was the horse's sex, but Hitchcock knew a sex change could make a witness's testimony worthless.

The men moved like rabbits, zigzagging and backtracking in order to conceal their activities and confuse anyone who might be trying to construct a sequence of events. During their travels, Smith, the leader of the trio, left the other two for days at a time. Madden and Hitchcock, however, stuck together, and Madden was present for each and every one of the horse trades Hitchcock made.

Before leaving New England, North Dakota, Hitchcock acquired a grey gelding from a young hotel worker, then he and Madden slowly headed back to Canada, crossing the border just southeast of Assiniboia, Saskatchewan. It was after dark when they arrived, about 10:00 p.m., and neither of them reported to Assiniboia customs.

Smith rejoined the two younger men, and the group made its way to the Scotsguard Livery Barn, where Hitchcock swapped his grey gelding for a young horse that needed to be broke and trained in order to be ridden — definitely not the most expeditious method of staying one step ahead of police! By this point, Madden, his mind reeling from all the horse swaps, left Smith and Hitchcock at the livery barn and went home.

Meanwhile, the liveryman, a fellow by the name of John Nordell, took Smith and Hitchcock into to his home and fed them supper. During the meal, Hitchcock told Nordell that he had got himself into "bad trouble" and that he'd "got the horse." Instead of contacting the authorities with this information, Nordell permitted Hitchcock to keep the stolen horse in his livery barn, loaned the young man his own horse, and then offered both Smith and Hitchcock employment.

Hitchcock, however, soon disappeared with Nordell's horse. Nobody saw or heard anything more from him until some time later, when Smith left Scotsguard for a week. When he returned, he had Nordell's horse. "I asked him where Hitchcock was," Nordell stated to police. "He told me [Hitchcock's] father was sick and had to go to the hospital and he couldn't come."

Though Hitchcock had disappeared, Smith agreed to work for Nordell, and soon enough, he and Harry Bolleson were pitching hay into the livery barn. That's when Smith said, "I'm looking for a buyer for a nice pair of horses that are downstairs."

"So I went in that night and bought the team from him," Bolleson later stated to police.

On October 11, 1915, less than a week after Constable Perry received the original telegram that something was amiss in Scotsguard, Birks arrested Smith at the livery barn.

On October 12, Hitchcock returned to Scotsguard and rode up to Madden's father's homestead. "I'm headin' to Oregon," he said to Madden. "I thought you might like to keep me company." As Madden considered the invitation, Hitchcock confided that police were pursuing both of them regarding some stolen horses.

With that news, Madden took off with Hitchcock, who was riding a bay mare with a white "L" on her face. A chestnut colt, only two months old, was being tagged along. This youngster, probably straight off its mother, had a silver mane and tail, as well as an angry wire cut on its left shoulder.

During their time in the saddle, Madden asked Hitchcock why police had come to be after them. "John Nordell of Scotsguard told me the police had arrested Smith, and were after me," explained Hitchcock. "Smith and I stole horses in the Pendleton area, you know, and now that they're after me, I'm changing my name. D'you think I look like a Charlie Davis?"

As Hitchcock pondered his name change, he and Madden continued riding away from the law. Hitchcock told Madden that he planned to sell his horses in Lethbridge, Alberta, then buy a train ticket and spend the winter in Spokane, Washington. Sometimes a rider's thoughts are never clearer than when he's in the saddle, and the more Madden thought about it, the less he wanted to be on the run. He wanted to go home to his father. Bidding Hitchcock good luck, he turned his horse around and rode back in the direction from which they'd come. Riding on alone, Hitchcock wondered if Madden might turn him in, especially now that he knew his plans. He thought about what he would say to the police if they caught up to him.

Madden wasn't home for long before he was questioned by Birks. He cooperated fully. Later, police were unflattering in their description of Madden: "...not overly gifted with brains, and seems to have a particularly poor memory." But poor memory or not, it was Madden's recollection of all the horse trades that police relied on to follow the thieves' trail.

Smith and Hitchcock were a masterful pair when it came to causing trouble for other people. In fact, once arrested, Smith accused Madden of stealing the goods he himself had been charged with stealing, namely the saddle he'd sold to Robert Stevenson, as well as the horse he'd been riding when he'd been arrested.

But various depositions revealed that it had indeed been Smith, posing as Ted Williams, who had sold the saddle to Robert Stevenson of Scotsguard for $20. Constable Birks brought a Mr. Tubbs all the way from Harlem, Montana, to determine whether or not the saddle — which had the number "44" stamped on its rear and a "4" stamped either side — was his. "The saddle … I identify positively as the saddle that was stolen from me at Harlem, Montana, by Art Smith last June," said Tubbs. "It is a penitentiary made saddle with peculiar swell and fork. The numbers burnt in the skirts and cantle have been placed there since the saddle was stolen." Tubbs then returned to Montana with his saddle, promising police that he would come back to Canada to appear against Smith at his trial.

But Smith kept his finger pointed squarely at poor Madden. He claimed that it was Madden and Hitchcock who were deeply engaged in horse trading, swapping one stolen horse for another, and that Madden had traded the stolen saddle for Smith's. "Four days below Assiniboia … Madden changed saddles with me," said Smith. "That is, he traded the Tubbs saddle to me for the saddle I had, as Tubbs' saddle made the back of his horse sore."

Madden admitted he knew the saddle Smith was talking about. He couldn't help but notice when other people had nice things. "It was a round skirted saddle," he recalled, then went on to describe its tall forks, narrow swell, and round bottom stirrups. Smith, attempting to raise the suspicions of police, drew their attention to how well Madden knew the saddle — but was that because he'd stolen it, or because he'd looked at it with envy? "It is the same saddle Art Smith had when he and Perrine Hitchcock caught up to me south of Harlem on June 17," Madden said. His young neck was on the line. How could he prove which of the three men had stolen the saddle?

Madden then made another statement to police. "Smith had this saddle in his possession all the time after we left Harlem, and brought it across the [border] with him. He had it and was using it when I left him and Hitchcock south west of Scotsguard and returned to my home ... I do not think there is another saddle made exactly like it," he said. "The saddle Smith got is a remarkable saddle."

When asked to describe the brands, Madden said, "There is 44 burnt in two places; on the back of the seat and one 4 on each skirt. I do not know who put them there. They were put there on the other side of Assiniboia ... The numbers on the skirt and cantle were burnt there after we crossed the line."

Authorities questioned Madden's innocence. Could he have stolen the horse and saddle after all? Or was Smith strategically employing the common criminal activity of accusing a naive teenager of his own crime, in hopes the teen would be convicted in his place?

Smith was prepared to elaborate to prove his innocence. "While we were cooking coffee, Madden went up to the CPR fence and cut off two pieces of wire and burned 4s on the Tubbs saddle, and M.S. on the other saddle, and also tried to make a brand, to brand that bay horse."

The accusation sounded plausible, and Smith made it more convincing to the authorities by adding, "A woman was standing in a car used as a living house and watched [Madden] cut the wire. We left there about 9 or 9:30 for Assiniboia. Madden changed saddles with me there."

Madden was beside himself. "I had nothing to do with burning 44 on the saddle. I do not know anything about it. I cut wire. I traded horses once. I had the same saddle right through," he told the justice. "I was hunting for my father's stock. We put up in shacks when we could get them. I never had the saddle of Tubbs unless the one Perrine gave me was his. I had my own saddle when I rode out of Harlem."

"It's a lie!" shouted Smith. "When we got back to Saskatchewan, I went straight to Perrine's place, and helped him shock hay, then I took Nordell's horse back to him, and worked there until I was unfairly arrested for bringing stolen property into Canada."

Stolen Horses

On November 17, 1915, Smith pleaded not guilty to two charges, one of bringing a stolen horse into Canada, the other of bringing a stolen saddle into the country. He elected for a speedy trial, and District Court Judge Smyth remanded him until the Crown prosecutor could fix a trial date.

Madden, meanwhile, was bound over in the sum of $2000 to appear as a witness at the trial. A warrant for Perrine Hitchcock was issued and held at the Shaunavon detachment of the RNWMP.

Smith's trial was held at Gull Lake, Saskatchewan, on December 15, 1915. He appeared before His Honour Judge Smyth. Evidence was the same as that provided at the preliminary hearing with one exception: the defence suggested that Charles Marsh, whose horse had been stolen by Smith after he had given him a ride into Harlem, Montana, had identified the wrong man. However, under cross-examination, Marsh looked at Smith and said, "I know you are the man, for I talked with you for 12 miles...you are the man that rode with me."

Judge Smyth found Art Smith guilty on both charges. Smith's attorney then suggested to the judge that in exchange for a suspended sentence, Smith would be willing to enlist in the army for active service. Judge Smyth acknowledged that while he had allowed prisoners who had been charged with minor offences to do this, he "would not care to risk such a man as the accused, charged with such a serious offence, to mingle with other men of good character." Judge Smyth also noted that this was, "one off the most flagrant cases I have ever had before me." He sentenced Smith to two years in Prince Albert Penitentiary.

Chapter 5
Fanfreluche

Her name was Fanfreluche and she was a national darling, the Canadian Horse of the Year in 1970. Her mother was multiple stakes winner Ciboulette, her father, the great Northern Dancer. Fanfreluche possessed astounding speed, amazing strength, and a competitive mentality. People around the racetrack began to whisper that she might even be able to do the amazing: race against the boys, and win.

Horse races are designed to be fair. Predictable performances are taken into consideration. For instance, young horses are pitted against young horses, and older ones against older ones. But within these predictions of performance is the limitation of sex. Female racehorses seldom have

64

the strength, stamina, and power needed to be serious contenders against stallions.

But Fanfreluche was different. Foaled in 1967, she came in the money an astounding 20 out of 21 racing starts from 1969 to 1970. A consistent stakes winner, she dominated events such as the Benson and Hedges Invitational and the Manitoba Centennial Derby. Her owner, Quebecor Jean-Louis Levesque, was convinced his "Fanny" would bring him what he coveted: the Queen's Plate.

First held in 1860, the Queen's Plate is one of the most prestigious horse races in Canada, and the oldest uninterrupted stakes race in North America. Over the years, many celebrated Thoroughbreds have run "the plate." Winning the race is a major accomplishment, resulting in both wealth and esteem for horse, trainer, and owner.

And in 1971, Fanfreluche had a shot at victory. Though her jockey, Chris Rogers, described the horse as a "chunky little filly," he believed that anyone who could overtake her would win the prestigious race. As one of only two fillies in a field of 15, she ran the two kilometres of the 111th Queen's Plate, finishing an exciting second — an astounding feat in a gruelling horse race of mixed sexes.

One of many outstanding Thoroughbred racehorses bred by Jean-Louis Levesque, Fanfreluche won $238,688 before she was four years old. She became a much sought-after broodmare. In the 1970s, owners of Thoroughbred racing mares dreamed of having their horses bred to the phenomenal Triple Crown stallion, Secretariat. Few mares, however, were deemed good enough to be bred by him. Fanfreluche was one of the exceptions. To Levesque's delight, she was soon in foal to Secretariat.

As a broodmare, Fanfreluche lived in enviable facilities in Paris, Kentucky, where she grazed in warm sunshine and received lavish care. Surprisingly, Levesque did not have her insured, either before or after her joining with Secretariat.

On June 27, 1977, horse racing fans throughout North America were stunned when they glanced at their morning papers. Without prior indication that anything was amiss, front-page headlines screamed the news, "Fanfreluche: Stolen!" She was two months into an 11-month gestation with Secretariat's foal. Reports variously placed her value at between $500,000 and $1.5 million. Levesque, the Kentucky police, and the FBI sat by the phone, waiting for a ransom call. The RCMP was called in on the investigation. Horse racing enthusiasts across the continent held their breath.

Last seen by a watchman in the late afternoon of June 25, Fanfreluche had been grazing with eight other brood-mares. When the watchman returned to do a head count that evening, he came up one head short. Assuming a horse was simply out of sight, he didn't look any further. As a result, it was the following morning before workers discovered a fence on the ranch had been tampered with, and that Fanfreluche was missing.

Many people speculated on the motive behind the theft

of the high-profile horse. Would she be bred, and her foals sold for a high price? This seemed unlikely; without a specific demand from the crooks, profits from selling Fanfreluche's foals would be severely limited at best. These foals would be unable to be registered, in which case, as "grade" foals, the youngsters would sell for a small fraction of their true value.

Perhaps Fanfreluche was stolen so that she could be raced under another name. But this, too, seemed doubtful. Regulatory racing agencies are careful about checking a horse's background at the best of times. And after a star horse is stolen, officials scrutinize every piece of paper and every horse that looks even remotely like the missing one. It seemed most likely that Fanfreluche's abductors were simply holding her for ransom. But surprisingly, no one attempted to contact Levesque to collect a ransom or make conditional demands.

As it turned out, the day after Fanfreluche went missing, farmer Harry McPherson came upon the Canadian darling walking along a road more than 240 kilometres from the sight of the theft. Exhausted and afraid, she was in sorry shape, with rope burns around her neck, behind her ears, and around her ankles. McPherson didn't recognize her as anything other than a poor old nag. He took her home, and when nobody came in search of her, he named her "Brandy."

Assuming "Brandy" was a riding horse, McPherson innocently restricted her grazing limits with a solitary strand of electrified wire. He fed her, took care of her, and gave her kindness — something she must have been grateful for after her ordeal.

Months passed. Ever hopeful that Fanfreluche was still alive, Levesque collaborated to post a $25,000 reward for the mare. Reward seekers soon directed investigators to McPherson's farm, where only one week earlier, he had declined a $200 offer for the horse.

Levesque and Fanfreluche were reunited, and less than three months later, she bore a stud colt. Levesque added a dash of magic to the celebrated event. He named the foal *Sain et Sauf*, French for "safe and sound."

The man convicted of Fanfreluche's theft was a horse trainer's grandson by the name of William Michael McCandless, also known as Michael McCandless and William Michael Rhodes. Described as a dreamer and a con artist, McCandless was a known gambler. Like most gamblers, he dreamed of the "big win."

Though details of how and why he was caught and charged with stealing Fanfreluche remain vague, McCandless was convicted of the theft in 1983 and sentenced to four years in jail. But by the 1990s, he was back to shady gambling, and at the age of 51, he was issued a six-count indictment for race fixing.

McCandless knew there were many ways a horse race could be fixed. In 1998, he was charged, in absentia, with engaging in one of the most unscrupulous of these ways: sponging. The process involved sticking a sponge up a horse's nostril and leaving it there. The "sponged" horses all lived in danger of inhaling the sponge beyond the nostril, contracting a serious infection, going into shock, or developing any number of autoimmune diseases as a result of ongoing rejection of the foreign object. They could also have collapsed during a race, causing death or serious injury to all race participants, human and horse. It has been assumed that cutting off a horse's air supply by this means was done in order to hurt the animal's performance and gain a gambling advantage.

The image of a Thoroughbred racehorse thundering round a track, grit flying at his face, nostrils flared and sucking air as he tries to meet the speed he's always had, the sting-sting-sting of the jockey's riding crop as the horse is urged to try harder, giving every last ounce he's got while an uncomfortable sponge presses against the delicate mucous membranes of his nose, blocking his airflow and reducing his oxygen supply, is unnerving. Each day, the sponge becomes increasingly clogged with body fluid, breeding millions of germs, crusting around the edges, and digging further into the animal's sensitive tissue.

McCandless was allegedly stuffing sponges up the nostrils of several horses in Kentucky. Although his intention may not have been to harm the horses, one horse, Class O' Lad, became a mortality statistic. During a race, Class O' Lad's jockey realized the horse was seriously distressed and, mercifully, pulled him up. Upon physical examination, sponges found up Class O' Lad's nostrils were believed to have caused him enough stress to develop laminitis, an agonizing and potentially fatal disease. Just six years old, Class O' Lad was euthanized.

The FBI began an investigation. Because of the potentially lethal result of sponging a horse, a $50,000 reward was offered in hopes that someone would come forward with the information needed to put a quick stop to it. McCandless was fingered for the crime, and though authorities did not know of his whereabouts at the time, he was indicted nevertheless.

Today, McCandless remains at large. Authorities continue to look for him A segment on McCandless was shown on the popular television program *America's Most Wanted*, but failed to produce the necessary information on his whereabouts.

Some people have questioned McCandless's guilt in both crimes, doubting his ability to pull off such feats. McCandless enjoyed a degree of recognition around the racetracks; many people knew him on sight. Some liked him and felt that if he was "sponging," then he must have been forced into it, or perhaps was taking the rap for someone else. His mother also remains convinced of his innocence of both crimes.

And what about Fanfreluche? She produced more foals, 20 in total, and five went on to become stakes winners. In 1999, she died at the impressive age of 32.

Chapter 6
Breeze and Vegas

On March 12, 1993, Delphine Crayford's father-in-law gave her a beautiful gift. He gave her three-year-old Breeze, a grey mare with four black legs, a black mane, and grey freckles on her face. A small horse, Breeze stood just over 15 hands high (five feet tall from the ground to the top of her withers). Due to her uncertain parentage, she was considered a grade horse rather than an identifiable purebred; her sire was believed to be a Quarter Horse, her maternal line was unknown. But while her parentage was uncertain, she was, and remains, an adored gift. "We just seemed to connect right off the bat," says Delphine, her voice gentle with affection. "She was a good little girl, so smart, a real quick learner."

Stolen Horses

Breeze is the grey on the left, Vegas is on the right

Rather than board Breeze at a riding stable, Delphine kept her right outside the back door, on the family's one-hectare property in Coleman, Alberta. In 1996, Breeze was given a friend in Vegas, a seven-year-old gelding that Delphine and her husband Gary bought for their five-year-old daughter. With a narrow chest and a white star on his forehead, Vegas — like Breeze — had no claim to pedigree blood. But also like Breeze, he quickly won his way into the Crayfords' hearts. "He was an awesome little horse," says Delphine. "He taught my daughter how to ride."

Both horses were regarded as members of the family.

Breeze and Vegas

They were ridden purely for the pleasure of it, and Breeze and Vegas always made it pleasurable. Five years after the horses first came to live on the Crayford property, they were even more loved than they had been in the early days of their arrival.

On June 25, 1998, a family friend drove past the Crayford property. She spotted someone in the front paddock with the horses. At first she thought it was Delphine's husband Gary, but quickly realized the man was too skinny to be him. As she passed the house, she looked over her shoulder to get a second look at the stranger. Unable to identify the man, she felt uneasy — but not uneasy enough to get nosy. Family members were often seen in the paddock with the horses, and lately, they were there more often than usual because Breeze had an infected hind foot that was being treated with penicillin. The neighbour continued to drive on to her own home a short distance away. Meanwhile Gary, a nightshift worker at that time, was upstairs in bed, asleep.

That night, everyone in the Crayford family was in bed by midnight. Delphine's two teenage daughters had both made it home for their 11 o'clock curfew, and when the doors were locked behind the girls, the horses were seen standing beside each other outside.

The following morning, Delphine was the first to get up. Venturing outside in her housecoat, she was surprised not to see the horses. She walked around the property and soon noticed that the back gate of the pasture was open. With mounting anxiety, Delphine ran through the open gate, then up the hill and across the pipeline, where she saw that the main gate was also open. Stunned, she rushed back to the house, phoned the police, and dressed quickly, alerting the rest of the family to her discovery as she did so.

Officers from two police departments — the RCMP and Crowsnest Pass Police —arrived at the Crayford house shortly after Delphine's call. Their investigations did not inspire confidence from the Crayfords. "The RCMP thought the horses were just 'out'," says Delphine. "They kept saying 'Oh, don't worry about it. They'll turn up'." But Delphine knew differently. "My horses are happy, and they don't open gates," she told one police officer.

Despite the lacklustre investigation, one officer did think it necessary to do a check of the rural pastures and try to get more information. However, when Delphine asked for the wide band at the top of her pasture gate to be finger-printed, police refused. The Crayfords sensed that authorities didn't think this was the theft of something valuable. "The minute it's an animal it's 'big deal'," says Delphine. Though one police officer found a witness in the area who claimed to have seen the horses being led up the road, the witness later recanted her statement. No reason was given for her contradiction, and authorities didn't press the matter for an explanation.

After the police left the Crayford house, the family, distraught and frustrated, walked together to the back of the property. As tears streamed down their faces, their shock and sense of loss was almost more than they could bear. Then they saw hoofprints on the ground.

"We found the tracks," recalls Delphine. "We followed them to a subdivision. We knew it was them because one horse was just putting the toe of the foot down." That track belonged to Delphine's beloved Breeze. Even with the pain of her infected foot, Breeze was gentle and kind, trying to keep her weight off her sore heel while walking obediently for her abductor. How the villain must have appreciated her sweet natured cooperativeness. A sudden burst of hope propelled the family forward as they followed the tracks. But their hearts quickly sunk when the hoofprints came to an abrupt end, and trailer marks took over. "They were loaded into a trailer…and then they were gone," says Delphine.

The next morning, the Crayfords rose early to begin another day of searching. Knowing it is not uncommon for stolen horses to be taken to slaughterhouses, Delphine and her family made their way to the nearest one, located an hour away in Fort MacLeod, Alberta. The slaughterhouse had a little holding pen where a person could drop a horse off after hours, putting the necessary paperwork through a slot in the door and leaving the horse in the pen. But Breeze and Vegas weren't there, and the Crayfords left the slaughterhouse to continue their pursuit.

Family friends came out to help with the search. A poster was quickly put together and taken to a local print shop, where 500 colour copies were printed. Website notices were posted, and a reward was offered for the return of the missing animals. The family also contacted the local media, phoned brand inspectors, and visited as many auction marts as they could. At a few of the auction marts, Delphine heard rumours that some brand inspectors would allow horses to go through the auction without proof of ownership. "I don't know if that was true," she says. Although sellers are supposed to prove ownership, a fake bill of sale would enable a thief to sell an animal that's not his or hers to sell.

About a week after Breeze and Vegas were stolen, a local radio station ran a feature on the horses and interviewed Delphine. Three weeks later, Delphine appeared on a morning television talk show, and soon after, a local news crew came out and filmed the area around the Crayford house for a segment on the thefts.

Then the leads started to come in. "Some leads were for ridiculous places," says Delphine, "but you have to check them all out. One lead turned out not to be even the right colour of horses!"

A livestock investigator in Calgary phoned Delphine after hearing her talk on the radio. Located mostly in Canada's western provinces, livestock investigators are government agents or law enforcement officers who check manifests for the proper number and description of animals, determine that brands do in fact belong to the person claiming ownership, and investigate missing livestock. The livestock investigator in Calgary suggested a few resources for Delphine, and put her in touch with a local police officer who was considered knowledgeable about rural affairs. The investigator then contacted a U.S. brand inspector (in case the thieves tried to take the horses across the border), and told Delphine that he believed the horses might have been seized by an organized crime element operating on a circuitous route from Calgary to Montana.

After the investigator's phone calls, the groundwork of the search had to be done by Delphine and her family. And sadly, even once this groundwork was done, the whereabouts of Breeze and Vegas were still unknown.

As the Crayfords continued to search for clues, Delphine's sister began to wonder if rodeo participants might have been involved. She had put some reining work into Breeze because Delphine was going to learn to rein. During the training time, Delphine's sister had used Breeze as an entry horse at the opening of a couple of rodeos. Had someone at the rodeo seen how adorable Breeze was, watched how easily she loaded into the trailer, and decided to steal her?

Of course, the thief could have been someone entirely outside of the rodeo, someone who was brazen enough to check the horses in their own pasture to see how approachable they were and how easy they would be to catch. Someone sinister and shameless enough to do this while Gary was asleep at only an arm's length away.

Three months after the horses disappeared, Delphine

began to consider contacting an animal communicator to help in the search. Delphine knew these specialists were contracted to perform a variety of services, most of which centred on communicating telepathically with an animal. She also knew that horse owners sometimes turned to animal communicators if their veterinarians were unable to identify a horse's specific ailment, and she had heard the testimonials claiming the communicators were often able to identify the condition. Some animal communicators say they are able to converse with animals regardless of whether the animas are dead or alive. Others claim only to speak with the living. And most claim that they can receive information from the animal while on the phone with the animal's owner.

Delphine had seen an animal communicator promoted on television, and the message suggested that this woman's services were affordable. For months, Delphine debated whether to contact her. Almost a year after the horses disappeared, she bit the bullet and phoned the animal communicator. But the cost proved to be much more than Delphine had expected. She was told that for $500 U.S. she could have half an hour on the phone with her. However, for a much smaller fee, she could ask two quick questions. Perhaps answers to two questions would be better than nothing.

Delphine agonized over how to phrase her two questions in order to get as much information as she could. Finally, she asked: "Do you know who took them?" The communicator answered that "Alice and Raymond" were responsible for taking Breeze and Vegas. Wondering how two first names would get her any closer to her horses, Delphine then asked, "Do you know where they are?" The communicator answered that the horses were in Butte, Montana.

Delphine hadn't thought it possible for the horses to be taken across the border. But, armed with the vague information the animal communicator had offered, she loaded her car up with posters, and the family headed off to Butte early on a Sunday morning. "It's an eight hour drive, and we had to be back that day," says Delphine, "so we didn't have much time to spend."

The family was able to visit with a brand inspector in Butte, but the visit did not bring much comfort. To their amazement, they learned it was actually easy to get a horse into the United States. With the border only two hours from the Crayford home, there were suddenly many new possibilities for Breeze and Vegas's whereabouts — new possibilities, but no new leads.

Only months after the family's visit to Butte, Delphine's suspicion that nobody appreciated the value of what had been stolen was reinforced. "I got a phone call from a female police officer," she explains. "She was retiring and wanted to tie up some loose ends, so she was closing the case. I told her that the case wasn't closed, the horses hadn't been found, but she insisted she wanted to tie up the loose ends."

Of course, tying up loose ends is something Delphine has been unable to do. "Not knowing means you have no closure…you don't get over it, " she says, her voice cracking. She still gets choked up when she drives past a grey horse in a field, wondering if it could be Breeze. "I've no idea what happened to the two of them. Maybe if the right person was to hear about the theft and be honest … maybe someday I'll be able to say, 'I got my horses back.' I'm still looking."

Chapter 7
Khalett

orse thieves do not limit themselves to stealing from pastures, barns, or stables to get their prizes. Most are perpetually alert for any opportunity they can exploit. Such an opportunity presented itself on Vancouver Island in the summer of 1997, when Darlene Gordon and her beloved horse Khalett went for a trail ride along a secluded logging road.

A beautiful Arabian mare, Khalett was born in 1983 on Darlene's 15 hectares in Courtenay, British Columbia. Darlene, who was present at the birth, combined the names of the foal's dam and sire; the Texan sire was River Song Khalid and the dam, Daodar Marett. Khalett's "bay" colouring meant that she was one of various shades of chestnut, accented with a black mane, muzzle, tail, and stockings.

As Khalett matured, Darlene decided to use her as a trail-riding horse, and she rode the mare in an old, unusual Toptani jumping saddle. Because her property was small, Darlene was always on the lookout for new places to ride. She didn't want Khalett to become bored with riding on the same paths all the time. The two travelled many new and interesting trails together. "She was a very good trail horse," remembers Darlene with obvious affection.

Accustomed to years of trail riding, Khalett had grown into a steady, dependable horse, always taking Darlene safely through new terrain, and enjoying the outings. In 1997, Khalett was 14 years old. The pair had been trail riding together for about a dozen years, and they were always happy to find new terrain and fresh trails to explore. On July 29, 1997, at about 6:00 p.m., Darlene loaded Khalett into her two-horse bumper pull trailer, and then drove to a new trail that she'd found about eight kilometres from home.

It was a beautiful sunny evening, and by 6:30 p.m., the two had started their ride on an old logging road surrounded by dense bush. The unfamiliar area resembled a tropical forest. "The growth was so dense that a person would have a hard time walking through it, let alone a horse," recalls Darlene. After riding for about an hour and a half, the pair came around a bend to find themselves facing — of all things — a flock of 30 emus! Making peculiar noises, the large birds

Khalett

began to approach Khalett and Darlene, causing Khalett to become fearful and restless. Darlene dismounted to try to scare off the birds and calm her horse. "If I'd have been smart, I'd have taken her away right away," says Darlene. Instead, as she tried to reassure the horse, Khalett suddenly bolted. Darlene lost her grip on the reins, and the horse ran back from whence she'd come. "I never saw her again," says Darlene.

Darlene followed Khalett by keeping an eye on the horse's hoofprints on the trail. She noted that for a short time, Khalett had run at a full gallop, then slowed down and eventually walked in the direction of Darlene's horse trailer. Hoping that Khalett might be waiting for her at the trailer, Darlene's concerns escalated when the hoofprints stopped at a water-filled ditch. Convinced that Khalett would not have jumped the ditch, Darlene began to wander around the unfamiliar area in search of her mare.

With no sign of the horse, Darlene returned to the logging road where she'd last seen the hoofprints. The road was lined with a few semi-isolated homes, and a handful of residents were milling around. Darlene asked if anyone had seen a riderless horse. "No one had seen her," recalls Darlene. "It's not as if they could have missed her. She was all saddled up, and her reins would've been flying."

Darlene was at a loss over where Khalett could have gone. The density of growth off the logging road was ideal for a cougar or small animal to hide in, but not for a horse to go through. "When a horse gets lost it's usually on a road, and they're found very quickly because there's no place for them to go," explains Darlene. "The bush is just too dense for them to go into."

When Darlene chose to head off and search in a certain direction, a couple of people standing along the road finally spoke up, saying that they'd seen the horse and that she'd gone a different way. Darlene went where they directed her, only to have other people along the road say the horse had taken another route. "You're running around looking for a horse and you know damned well that people are lying to you because she didn't vanish into thin air."

Darlene grew increasingly frustrated and panicked. She was running around in circles, and the residents on the trails were controlling the direction in which she travelled. "I think these people kept trying to get me to go in the opposite direction. They were not nice people," she says. "But how many times do you expect people to steal your horse? It's inconceivable to me, but obviously they must have known where she was. If I'd been where there were no people around, I think I'd have gone where I thought she was, and found her."

Khalett's hoofprints at the water-filled ditch suggested that she'd milled around that one spot for probably several minutes. Darlene wondered if someone had come up to Khalett, taken the lead rope, and led her away. "There could only have been about 15 minutes between the time she got to that spot and the time that I did," she explains. "She had to have been just led off to the bush and held there, watching me while I was worried that she'd carried on and would get into traffic. [The thieves] were opportunists because [they] could see me running around, frantic."

At one point, two young men who were hanging around asked Darlene if there was a reward for finding the horse. But she hadn't even reached that stage of thought. "I did think it was a bit strange to ask about a reward for a horse that was supposedly just down the road a bit," she says. "When I look back, I should've said 'yes' and I wonder if I'd said that if it would've made a difference."

By 11 o'clock that night, Darlene was exhausted; she drove home with her empty horse trailer. In total disbelief, she grew more and more certain that Khalett had been stolen, and that the thieves were keeping her out of sight from searching eyes. "I was hoping I was wrong, but why couldn't I find her?" she still asks. "It was really upsetting and terrible. They used to *hang* people for this!"

As she drove onto her property, her spirits sunk even more. "I was exhausted," she remembers, her voice breaking. "I had been walking around and was really strung out, and the other horses came running over, whinnying to welcome [Khalett] home, and she wasn't there."

Darlene fed her dogs then tried to sleep. Up at 4:30 the next morning, she phoned some friends who came to help her look for the horse. She phoned auction houses and people who trailer horses from one location to another. One generous man hired a helicopter to go up and look for Khalett. Another friend brought his own dependable trail horse along to search the trials and possibly draw Khalett out of the bush in the event that she was hiding. However, when this horse refused to cross the water-filled ditch, Darlene became even more certain that Khalett hadn't gone over it either. She distributed flyers, and on them, indicated that a reward was being offered. The amount wasn't stipulated. A few days later, a friend contacted the RCMP on Darlene's behalf. "He said the police were really reluctant to bother," she remembers. "I think it might have been a little different if she'd been stolen out of the field." However reluctantly, police did open a file on the horse.

Soon after Khalett's disappearance, rumours about a dead horse in the area began to circulate. But no one ever contacted Darlene personally about such a find. The stories always came third or fourth-hand from hunters or surveyors. Worse, residents along the logging road kept insisting that Khalett was nowhere to be found. "I think they knew who had her but didn't want to say anything," says Darlene. Sometimes she would bump into people who knew her horse was missing, and they would say: "Oh, I heard you found your mare dead." But none of these people ever actually enquired about the source of this news. "It would have been better if I had found her dead," Darlene says. "At least I'd have known where she was."

By early August of 1997, Darlene realized her horse could be anywhere. She knew that British Columbia auction houses did not require proof of ownership to sell a horse; Khalett could have passed through an auction house as an unregistered — but flashy — Arabian, and no one would have raised an eyebrow. Added to this setback was the fact that Darlene lived on Vancouver Island. The horse could easily have been loaded into a horse trailer, driven onto the ferry, and ended up on the mainland to be sold there without question.

For the next month, Darlene kept looking, receiving countless false leads along the way. She received phone calls from people saying they'd seen the horse weeks before, but didn't know where the animal was now; and from people saying they'd seen the horse in the southern U.S., or Montreal, or any other assortment of places. One call from British Columbia's interior sounded promising. The people who made the call subsequently convinced the RCMP to investigate. "A female officer went up but didn't see the horse," says Darlene. Oddly, during the conversation with police, the suspects implied that they knew Darlene well, and that they had purchased a buckskin mare from her. But Darlene has never owned — or sold — a buckskin horse.

Hoping to draw the necessary information that would allow her to find her horse, Darlene put up a web page and posted a $1000 reward. Lots of people visited the website, and for a long time, Darlene opened up the abundant e-mails generated by the visits, eager to find a diamond lead. "Mostly it was just idiots making stupid statements, or else it was kindly folks who were sympathetic, but unfortunately couldn't help," says Darlene. People e-mailed her from as far away as California, often telling stories that only served to etch her wounds deeper.

Darlene realized that with the passage of time, it was becoming less likely that Khalett would be returned; the longer the horse was missing, the harder it would be for someone to return the animal without admitting some complicity in her disappearance. Darlene decided to make the risk worth it. She upped the reward to $10,000. "I would have had a bit of trouble coming up with that amount, but thought it would be worth it if it brought a chance of recovering her, or at least knowing where she was."

And, even though she didn't believe in the power of psychics, Darlene called one. "The reading was so vague it was impossible to follow. Some cowboy had her on the coast. It was useless, but I had to try," she says. Friends who also believed they possessed psychic abilities told her that Khalett was in a specific field, but when they went to the spot, the horse wasn't there. "I would get this hope up, and then it would be dashed. It was like getting kicked in the face again."

One small consolation was received much later. Darlene drove through Fort McLeod and stopped off at the slaughterhouse. Even though no one could help her, Khalett's picture was still posted in the office with her information, including a notation about a fungal infection that had been evident on the animal's lower legs — not a serious infection, more of a nuisance thing. Darlene hoped that if Khalett had found her way to caring people, that they might get a veterinarian to look at the infection, and the vet might ultimately help return her to her rightful owner.

Eventually, after newspaper, magazine, radio, and television coverage of Khalett's disappearance failed to turn up the horse, and after having spent several hundred dollars in advertising and posters, Darlene concluded that she was unlikely to ever see Khalett again. She never believed such a nightmare could happen. "It made me a little disgusted with some people, and a lot less trusting than I used to be," she says. "It's so upsetting. I was lied to, to my face. But I still think about Khalett and wonder what happened to her, or if she's even still alive."

An avid and frequent rider before Khalett's disappearance, Darlene has not ridden the trails since she lost her horse. Despite how much she used to love horses and riding, she has now given up everything that has to do with them. "Better to sell the horses and know what happened to them, than this," she explains sadly. She has sold her horse trailer and all but one of her remaining horses, a Morab gelding who reminds Darlene of Khalett. His sale will be completed soon.

Six years after Khalett's disappearance, Darlene still thinks about her and wonders what fate awaited the animal. "I still involuntarily look for her when I go past a field of horses," she says. "It has been an upsetting few years. Not knowing is the worst."

And the nightmare of not knowing has been compounded by the fact that Darlene believes there are people out there who do know what happened to her mare. "The other bad thing is knowing that someone knows but has deliberately not told me," she says. "Some evil person who doesn't know me, and I have no idea why they'd want to be so hurtful."

Chapter 8
Mekeezun

In the late summer of 2000, an American Paint Horse named Mekeezun was nibbling Alberta grass when she was purchased by Christine Pohlkamp of Guelph, Ontario. Christine had gone though the usual long-distance purchase procedure, making phone calls, seeing videotapes of the horse in action, but never actually meeting the animal. The fact that seven-year-old Mekeezun was in foal with her first baby was a mixed blessing. Christine wasn't a breeder. She just wanted a nice, flashy horse to ride.

And Mekeezun was flashy. When she arrived in Guelph by horse trailer, she was heavy in foal, but Christine fell in love with her on sight. Mekeezun's unique black and white markings on her left shoulder looked very much like an inverted map of Italy, a feature that led to her name, which is Ojibway for "the boot." She also sported a nifty little brand, low on her right flank, which looked like the roof of a house overtop a circle.

Soon after her arrival, Mekeezun dropped her foal on the ground. Christine witnessed the birth, a process that touched her deeply on both an emotional and spiritual level. Thinking that her work was over, Mekeezun demonstrated her gentle disposition not by standing protectively over her foal, but by being warm and sociable to anyone who came around to see the new baby. Mekeezun's large, round brown eyes endeared her to everyone who showed up.

Despite Christine's original intention to have a riding horse, it wasn't long before Mekeezun was in foal again. She carried the growing life for the mandatory 11 months or so, then, once again, dropped the foal in front of Christine and went off to hang around with nearby humans.

Soon after the second birth, Christine felt the urge to own a Friesian horse. She knew that Friesians were expensive. When her finances wouldn't stretch far enough for the horse she wanted, Christine decided to breed Mekeezun to a Friesian stallion. This was to be the mare's last foal before becoming a full-time riding horse.

With her two previous foals, Mekeezun's sides had expanded as the fetuses grew. But with the half-Friesian fetus, her sides didn't expand much. Instead, her belly kept getting closer to the ground, making her look more sway-backed than pregnant. But Mekeezun didn't appear laboured with the fetal position, and carried on as usual.

Christine was eager for the birth of this foal, an event due to take place at the end of March 2003. A few weeks before each of Mekeezun's prior deliveries, Christine had taken the mare from her home to a foaling stable about 15 kilometres away. Due to the delicate disposition of horses, pregnant mares need to be monitored carefully when they go into labour. Foaling stables provide extra roomy stalls, as well as specialized food and careful monitoring, prior to and following the delivery. Attendants watch the mares for signs of impending labour, and once these signs are observed, the mare is taken to her stall. There she is monitored 24 hours a day by way of cameras discretely hooked up inside the stall. The cameras avoid disturbing the mare in her early stages of labour while relaying a clear picture of the horse and the progression of the labour to the attendants.

Christine liked the foaling stable that Mekeezun had been to for the previous pregnancies. She liked the caring, watchful attendants, and she was happy with the way Mekeezun and her foals had been tended. So, not surprisingly, she opted to bring the mare to the same place a couple of months before she was due to drop the Friesian cross.

During her times of "confinement," Mekeezun had befriended another broodmare, Spot, who delivered her foals around the same time as Mekeezun. The two pastured together, and in the barn, were stalled directly across from each other. The stalls were large enough to house a full-grown horse and her rapidly growing youngster. The front wall of each stall had a dual purpose. On the inside, the wall served to enclose the front of the stall, providing safety, privacy, and shelter from drafts coming through the barn on windy days. On the outside, it was the barrier of the aisle that stretched through the length of the barn. A steel gate across the entrance to the stall prevented the horse or foal from getting out; once closed, the heavy, hinged gate locked securely with a dowel-shaped lock.

As she had before, Mekeezun settled in quickly at the foaling stable, perhaps because once again, Spot was there, too. Two or three times a week, during the coldest days of winter, Christine drove to the stable to groom and exercise the mare. She attached a lead shank to MeKeezun's halter, and the two of them walked outside in the nippy air, their feet crunching the snow in a two-step, four-step rhythm, and their breath making puffy white clouds as they exhaled. During these exercise sessions, Christine talked to Mekeezun, telling her stories about what the animals at home were doing, and of course, how much she was looking forward to the arrival of the foal.

Sometimes, when Christine brushed the mare, she gently laid her head against the horse's belly, hoping to hear or feel some indication that the foal was alive and well. And as she gave, so she received: once, as she listened for the baby, she was kicked squarely in the head by the foal!

Less than a week before Meekezun was due to foal, Christine had to go to Halifax, Nova Scotia, on business. She visited the mare before she left. "It was Wednesday, and it was really cold. I told her, 'don't have your baby while I'm gone! I'll be back two days before you're due to foal. Wait for me!'" With that, Christine left for the East Coast.

The evening of Saturday, March 22, was cold and dark. At 7:00 p.m., the stable owner brought Mekeezun into the barn and locked her in her stall for the night. Mekeezun looked across the aisle at Spot while the owner put grain in their buckets. Then each horse buried her head in her respective pail and chewed rhythmically. As the two mares ate their grain, they periodically leaned over to look across the aisle at each other.

The stable owner inspected each of the horses. Mekeezun's udders were "waxing up," a sure sign that foaling would take place within the next three or four days. The drama of birth was starting to unfold, but a bigger drama was about to begin.

One hour later, the owner made a safety check. When she entered the barn, she knew immediately that something was wrong. The gate to Mekeezun's stall was on the floor. The stall was empty. The woman frantically searched through the barn, but to no avail.

Because Christine was out of town, her partner, Grant Robertson, and a mutual friend were called. With a slew of other people, they searched for the horses on foot and by ATV until 2:00 a.m., combing the back roads and trudging through frozen swamp. Later that morning, a number of Christine and Grant's friends went looking on horseback, paying special attention to farms that were home to other horses in case the mare had uncharacteristically gone "visiting."

The following day, the Ontario Provincial Police were called in. As everyone searched, someone found hoofprints, wide and shoeless, in the dirt on the road near the foaling stable. The hoofprints circled the tire tracks of a truck and trailer.

Christine was oblivious to the ongoing panic and potential danger her horse was in. When Grant picked her up from the airport the next day, he said, "I've got something to tell you. We have to talk." When they arrived home, Grant sat her on the side of the bed and gently told her, "Mekeezun is missing."

Christine promptly went into shock. "My heart just stopped," she says. Her mind racing, she wondered if the mare could have given birth standing, tied up in a trailer. The very thought gave her chills. "It felt like … a personal attack. It was so traumatic and awful. People have no idea," she says.

While the search for Mekeezun continued, police asked Christine if she could think of anybody who might have had something against her. But neither she nor Grant could think of anyone. Christine's frustration mounted when one of the officers informed her that they couldn't broadcast

Mekeezun's brand or markings on the police computer system. "He said, 'If she had a tattoo we'd send out the number,' but because she doesn't have a tattoo, he wouldn't," Christine recalls, shaking her head. "I told him that her brand is easy to describe, just like a child's clothing, and he said, 'It's not a child'."

While Mekeezun's whereabouts remained unknown, everyone tried to fit the pieces of the puzzle together. It was hard to imagine how the horse could have lifted the heavy steel gate off its hinges. For safety reasons, there were no ledges or gaps that the horse could have used for leverage. The stall bore no evidence of struggle that might suggest another animal had come into the barn and frightened the mare.

Could Mekeezun have simply gone off somewhere to have her foal alone? With a history of quiet foaling, there was no reason to believe she would have taken such drastic measures to do this. Besides, her grain was still in the feed bucket, and a pregnant mare, in all likelihood, would devour that grain unless a serious force — like a human — had taken her away from it. Then there were those tire marks and hoofprints to consider. And so, Christine found herself with an unsettling mystery and a huge hole in her life.

On Tuesday, March 25, Christine was giving a business-related workshop when she received three messages on her cellular telephone, all in quick succession. The first message was from her veterinarian's wife. The message said, "We've found your mare and foal, and the foal's in distress."

Anxiously, Christine listened to the second message: "We've found your mare and the baby's okay." The third message said: "We found your mare and foal, and since we can't reach you, we've called the owner of the foaling barn, who's coming out to get them."

Within half an hour Mekeezun and her little filly foal were loaded into a trailer and driven back to the foaling barn. Christine's veterinarian inspected both animals and performed a postnatal examination. He estimated that the foal had been born the previous day. Once again Christine was thrown into an emotional upheaval. Where and how was Mekeezun found?

As it turned out, she was discovered two concessions and three kilometres away from the foaling farm. A woman who worked at a training stable had gone out to bring in their horses when she spotted Mekeezun with her foal in the field. She knew instantly the mare didn't belong on the property. "This property had been searched several times for Mekeezun," explains Christine. "A flyer that had been posted on the bulletin board of the barn instructed where to call in the event the horse was found."

Though relieved that Mekeezun and the foal were safe, Christine couldn't help feeling some regret as well. "I missed out on the birth," she says. "I was present for all of the pregnancy and every vet test, and I didn't get to see the baby being born. It still makes me mad that [the thief] took that away from me."

Mekeezun

She is also plagued by unanswered questions. "I sometimes wonder if whoever took her didn't realize that she was pregnant until after they took her. She was completely clean when she was found. There was no mud, or leaves, or anything on either her or the foal, which leads [me] to believe that she foaled in a barn."

Of course, it's possible that whoever took Mekeezun didn't realize until after the fact that she'd be difficult to unload. The horse's distinctive markings were easily recognizable, and her small brand would not have gone unnoticed at an auction sale. Without proper documentation, proving ownership of the horse could have been difficult.

And how would a thief have explained the foal? It's possible that whoever picked Mekeezun up hadn't known she was in foal, or if they had, hoped to find a purebred Paint foal on the ground instead of a strange looking crossbred foal of a solid colour. Perhaps the thief or thieves just got scared, and decided to leave the horse somewhere in hopes that people would think she'd somehow been overlooked during the search.

Whatever the case, as soon as Mekeezun was found, police closed the investigation. "I asked them to continue looking for the thief, but they refused," says Christine, shaking her head in disbelief.

A local newspaper reported that Mekeezun had been found and was safely home. But was she unscarred? Historically, Mekeezun had always been willing to share her babies with other horses and humans. "When she first came back, she was a bit skittish," says Christine. "She wasn't as social. She was reluctant to be touched or even brushed, and would walk away. It took about a month and a half for this to settle. She wasn't like this with either of her other foals. I would say this traumatized her."

If horses could talk, Christine would know for sure how the horsenapping affected Mekeezun. Horses do have mental flashbacks; unpleasant experiences are readily recalled by a sight, sound, or smell they associate with a bad time. But until more information about the theft can be found, no one knows whether the mare was treated well or poorly. Mekeezun is quietly holding on to the information that only she and her abductors know.

"It still bothers me," says Christine, gulping hard. "Just talking about it bothers me. I wish I knew who did it because I've got a big issue with him … I still get nightmares."

Bibliographic Note

John McEvoy has additional details about the Fanfreluche theft in his book, *Great Horse Racing Mysteries*, published by The Blood-Horse Inc., Lexington, Kentucky.

Acknowledgments

My sincere thanks to those people who endured the hardship of recalling their arduous experiences with horse theft so that this book could be written: Delphine Crayford, Darlene Gordon, and Christine Pohlkamp.

Thanks to the RCMP, and to Ontario Premier Ernie Eves's staff for considering my deadline. Thanks also to The National Archives of Canada, and the *Toronto Star*. All quotes found in the first four chapters of this book were taken directly from historical police reports, and those in the Fanfreluche chapter were taken from the *Toronto Star* archives.

Finally, thanks to the following people: Rossie historian Sandra Wyman, for her colourful details and added extras; Sandra Phinney, for her support and friendship, which I cherish; Dan Streeter, for his willingness to teach me how to do better, his patience and friendship. You're the best! And lastly, to Kara Turner and Jill Foran, for trusting me to deliver.

About the Author

Dorothy Pedersen has worked in various facets of the horse industry for over 20 years. An award-winning writer and public speaker, she holds an honours diploma in equine studies, as well as a certificate of horsemanship.

After having her own horses stolen in 1992, Dorothy undertook extensive research into the crime of horse theft, and has continued to investigate this aspect of crime — including its prevention and detection — ever since. She has had articles on horse and livestock theft published throughout North America for 15 years, and has been told by two government sources that she probably knows more about this crime than anyone else in the country. In 1996, she was asked to consult with the Ontario Provincial Police, and provided the information that led to the creation of their livestock database.

She is currently drafting her next writing project, a handbook on livestock theft prevention and detection. Dorothy lives in Grand Valley, Ontario, and owns a fully retired horse.

Photo Credits

Cover: Dorothy Pedersen; **Darlene Gordon:** page 83; **Delphine Crayford:** page 72.

RIDING ON THE WILD SIDE
Tales of Adventure in the Canadian West

"Suddenly, there was a crashing noise to our left and out of the timber came about 20 head of horses and a few bewildered elk followed by a couple of yelling cowboys."

This fascinating collection of stories is about working horses and the people who make a living riding them in Canada's mountain national parks. Imagine chasing a herd of wild horses, galloping at full speed toward an impenetrable forest ... and you get a sense of the excitement of the backcountry life.

 True stories. Truly Canadian.

ISBN 1-55153-985-3

AMAZING STORIES

ALSO AVAILABLE!

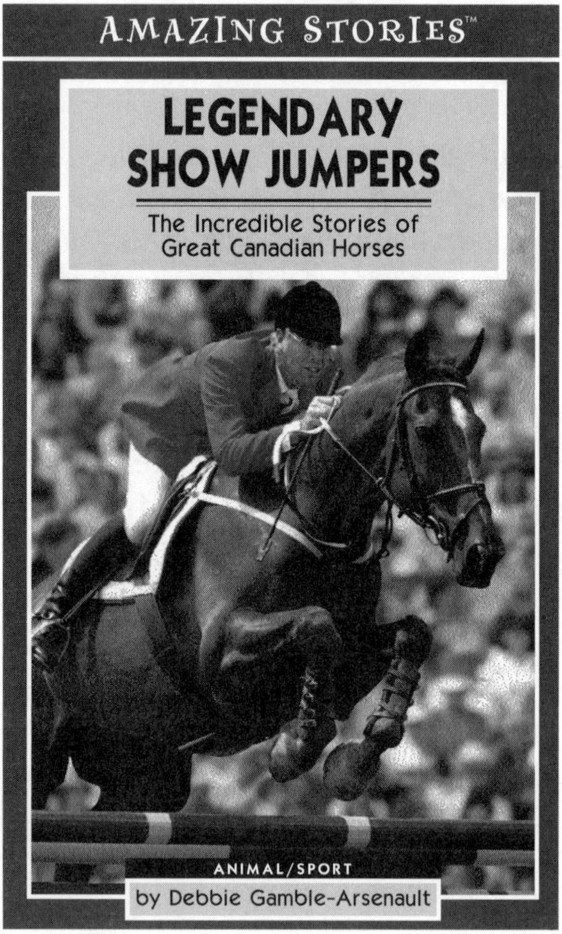

LEGENDARY SHOW JUMPERS
The Incredible Stories of Great Canadian Horses

"He could be so gentle and quiet, but when he got in the ring he got so excited we couldn't hold him. ...But I wasn't afraid of him."
Louis Welsh on Barra Lad

Once in a while a horse comes along that is extraordinary. Air Pilot, Barra Lad, and Big Ben have all had their turn at being the brightest star blazing in the show-jumping sky. For more than 100 years, great Canadian high-flying horses have provided spectators with exhilarating displays of their jaw-dropping talent and love of jumping.

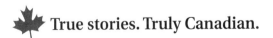 True stories. Truly Canadian.

ISBN 1-55153-980-2

THE HEART OF A HORSE
Poignant Tales and Humorous Escapades

"With the first jump, I would be trying to bring that old pony's head up and around to stop him. By the second jump, I was already looking for the perfect place to land. By the third jump I had mentally said my 'Goodbye Cruel World' speech. By the fourth I was picking dirt out from between my teeth."

This collection of heart-warming tales of one woman's passion for horses covers the spectrum from breeding and training, to adventures involving grizzly bears, uncooperative cows, and a truck named Herman. Gayle Bunney's comic insights bring to life the wild and wonderful experience of living with horses.

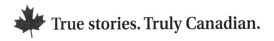 True stories. Truly Canadian.

ISBN 1-55153-994-2

OTHER AMAZING STORIES

These titles are available wherever you buy books. If you have trouble finding the book you want, call the Altitude order desk at **1-800-957-6888**, e-mail your request to: **orderdesk@altitudepublishing.com** or visit our Web site **at www.amazingstories.ca**

New AMAZING STORIES titles are published every month.

Comments on other *Amazing Stories* from readers & reviewers

"Tightly written volumes filled with lots of wit and humour about famous and infamous Canadians."
Eric Shackleton, *The Globe and Mail*

"The heightened sense of drama and intrigue, combined with a good dose of human interest is what sets Amazing Stories *apart."*
Pamela Klaffke, *Calgary Herald*

"This is popular history as it should be... For this price, buy two and give one to a friend."
Terry Cook, a reader from Ottawa, on **Rebel Women**

"Glasner creates the moment of the explosion itself in graphic detail...she builds detail upon gruesome detail to create a convincingly authentic picture."
Peggy McKinnon, *The Sunday Herald,* on **The Halifax Explosion**

"It was wonderful...I found I could not put it down. I was sorry when it was completed."
Dorothy F. from Manitoba on **Marie-Anne Lagimodière**

"Stories are rich in description, and bristle with a clever, stylish realness."
Mark Weber, *Central Alberta Advisor,* on **Ghost Town Stories II**

"A compelling read. Bertin...has selected only the most intriguing tales, which she narrates with a wealth of detail."
Joyce Glasner, *New Brunswick Reader,* on **Strange Events**

"The resulting book is one readers will want to share with all the women in their lives."
Lynn Martel, *Rocky Mountain Outlook,* on **Women Explorers**

THE HEART
OF A HORSE

AMAZING STORIES

THE HEART OF A HORSE

Poignant Tales and Humorous Escapades

ANIMAL/HUMAN INTEREST
by Gayle Bunney

PUBLISHED BY ALTITUDE PUBLISHING CANADA LTD.
1500 Railway Avenue, Canmore, Alberta T1W 1P6
www.altitudepublishing.com
1-800-957-6888

Extreme care has been taken to ensure that all information presented in
this book is accurate and up to date. Neither the author nor the
publisher can be held responsible for any errors.

Publisher   Stephen Hutchings
Associate Publisher   Kara Turner
Editor   Frances Purslow

We acknowledge the financial support of the Government
of Canada through the Book Publishing Industry Development
Program (BPIDP) for our publishing activities.

Altitude GreenTree Program
Altitude Publishing will plant twice as many trees as were used
in the manufacturing of this product.

National Library of Canada Cataloguing in Publication Data

Bunney, Gayle, 1954-
Heart of a Horse / Gayle Bunney

(Amazing stories)
ISBN 1-55153-994-2

Horse--Anecdotes. 2. Bunney, Gayle, 1954- --Anecdotes. I. Purslow,
Frances. II. Title. III. Amazing stories (Canmore, Alta.)
SF301.B852 2003   636.1   C2003-910419-2

An application for the trademark for Amazing Stories™
has been made and the registered trademark is pending.

Printed and bound in Canada by Friesens
4 6 8 9 7 5

For two young horse lovers who have worked beside me out in the horse corrals. While learning about the care and control of our faithful friend, the horse, they gave me joy and laughter and made me young at heart again. Thank you, Amanda Wager and Travis Minor.

The author getting ready for another day of ranch work.

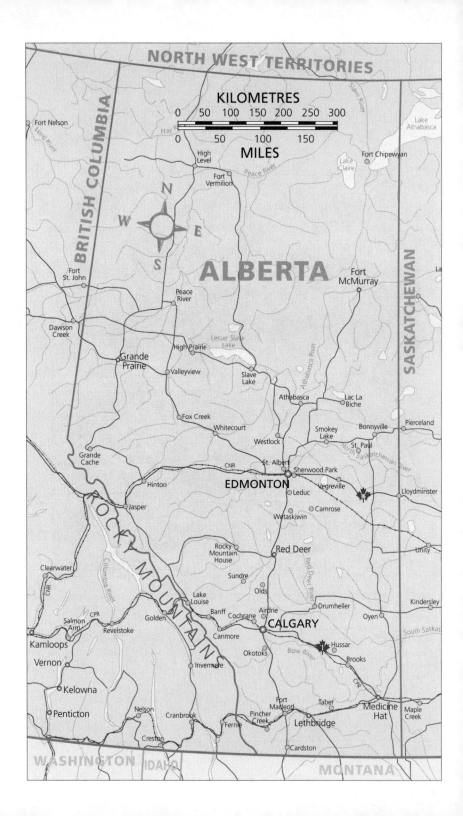

Contents

Prologue

Today is already cracking up to be just another typical day at my acreage. One of my many dogs woke me early by placing two muddy paws on my forehead. The farrier arrived ahead of schedule to trim the horses' feet and put an end to my morning coffee. After catching and tying the first half dozen horses along the fence for him, I thought fleetingly about eggs and toast, but a gelding that hasn't recovered after a complicated surgery needed to be doctored first.

The farrier is fast and, by the time I put away the vet supplies, is patiently waiting for more horses to be caught. My stomach makes its first loud complaint, but a man coming to purchase one of my two year olds is expected before noon, and I want to trim its mane before he arrives. I might as well catch the well-trained sorrel at the same time. I will saddle both of them. I suspect after the buyer has ridden both the green colt and the trained sorrel, he may cough up the extra money to buy the super quiet sorrel that doesn't need weeks' more training.

The farrier trudges by me, halter in hand. He will catch the old broodmares himself. It's probably quicker than waiting on the owner, who is having trouble catching the well-trained but wild-eyed and snorting sorrel.

The Heart of a Horse

I shake the buyer's hand as he gets out of his truck and head him towards the main corral. I wonder why he gives me such an odd look. I turn to write out the cheque for the farrier. A man of few words, the farrier slips silently into his truck. But he can't resist. Rolling his window down, he says what he has secretly been wanting to say all morning: "Why do you have two perfect muddy paw prints on your forehead?" And you know what? It's not even noon yet.

Chapter 1
Flashlights and Glowing Eyes

am late getting out to do the night grain feeding for the horses. They stomp and nicker as I head towards the corrals. I inch my way towards them, trying not to trip in the dark on the dozen excited miniature dogs around my feet.

Sure enough, my toe lands on someone's tail and the horrendous screeching that ensues makes my hair stand on end. I mutter that I should have docked its tail as a puppy so things like this wouldn't happen. I reach the light pole and flip the switch. Instantly the yard lights up. But five steps from the power pole, I hear a strange sizzling sound overhead. Two more steps and with a distinct popping sound, the yard light burns out, plunging me back into total darkness. Oh great, just great.

After fumbling with the safety chain on the main corral gate, I get it open and am met with a pen full of hungry weanlings pushing around me. I assure them that since they have the best of hay in front of them 24 hours a day, I doubt very much being two hours late with their grain is going to kill them. In response, one stud colt nips me smartly on the sleeve, managing to get some of my skin, too. Now I am showing the dog with the sore tail what real screeching sounds like. Ouch, that hurt. If I knew for sure which colt had done the dirty deed, I would bite him back.

The weanlings are all fed and accounted for. Both stallions are fed and accounted for. The mares and fillies are fed but I have to recount because one appears to be missing in the dark. Three recounts and one is definitely missing. It is a black yearling filly. No normal yearling would ever be off by herself. An old mare may go off by herself in the pasture, but not a young horse out of sight of the herd unless…. Lord, she is either sick or tangled in a fence. Back to the house on the double for a flashlight.

Strangely the pack of dogs only follow me as far as the pasture gate, then they beat it back towards the house. Man's best friend just deserted me. I head out down the centre of the pasture, stopping to call the filly's name and listen for any sounds in return. No whinnies, no twanging wire, no soft thud of hooves, nothing.

Flashlights and Glowing Eyes

Halfway across the pasture, the thin beam of the flashlight picks up the glint of eyes to the south. I steady the light on the eyes. The filly must be lying down judging from the height of the glowing eyes off the ground. Speaking quietly, and pointing the light towards the ground to avoid panicking her, I head towards the filly. After several yards, I again shine my light towards her to make sure I am heading in the right direction. Suddenly, the glowing eyes go straight up in the air. "That's good," I think. "She can't be too sick if she can get to her feet." I turn off the flashlight because her head held up that high may be a sign she's getting spooked. I sure don't want her to turn and hit the fence behind her.

I walk more slowly, almost singing a flow of gentle words to keep her calm and let her know she has nothing to fear. Because I am forced to zigzag around rocks and dips in the land, I chance another quick look at her with the light. She is lying down again. This is not good at all. But wait! If she is lying down how come she is moving towards me? Now her glowing eyes have shot straight up in the air again. All of a sudden she is back down again. What is going on? That is the last time I eat four-day-old pizza for supper. My brain must be suffering from some kind of food poisoning.

Suddenly from the north side of the small pasture, comes the crashing of an animal charging through the willows. I am consumed by fear — fear of the approaching glowing eyes and fear of the animal careening towards me. I am frozen to the spot, as frozen as a turkey in the deepfreeze waiting for Thanksgiving.

Just then, the owner of the glowing eyes decides to give a warning woofing noise. Lord Love-a-duck, it's a bear! Scant yards in front of me, and coming my way. I realize that when those glowing eyes went high in the air, it was the bear rearing up on his hind legs to better see the idiot human walking straight to his waiting jaws. From the north comes the shrill whinny of the frightened missing yearling.

This frozen turkey suddenly sprouts wings, and I am out of there. I fly over the ground, going wide open. But the bear is gaining on me fast. I hear his thundering stride, and I'm terrified that I'm not going to make it back to the safety of the yard. It's all over. The open gate looms before me, but I can feel the bear gaining on me. I try for one last burst of speed.

As the black filly passes me and swerves through the gate ahead of me, I no longer hear the thunder of the charging bear's feet behind me. Silly me, since when do bear paws go "clippity clop, clippity clop?" Obviously, the bear couldn't be bothered to try and catch this frightened morsel of chicken.

Chapter 2
The Horse That Came to Stay

Socks was a pretty nice gelding. Nice enough that buyers were always interested in him. That made my job of buying, training, and selling a whole lot easier.

I had purchased him as an unhandled two year old. His only close contact with humans had been getting dumped on the ground, gelded, and branded. He was a bit wild-eyed in the sale ring and scruffy enough looking that I didn't have to go overboard on the price paid for him. Once home, I gave him a healthy dose of dewormer, some good quality feed, and in no time he was looking pretty sharp. He took to being halter broke like a mouse to church on Easter Sunday. He took to the first saddling like he was born to wear a saddle. He took to training like a dog takes to a bone. He was good enough quality to keep around for a full year and finish his training. But Socks had some annoying habits. Although he was as gentle as a kitten, he always managed to step on my toes — especially if I went to the corrals wearing running shoes instead of boots. The pain is more intense with only $9 running shoes between you and the horse's hoof instead of a pair of sturdy cowboy boots. As well, he always decided to bite at that horsefly on his side just as I was bending down to pick up a front hoof to clean it. WHAM! When our heads connected, I was the loser. Also, he'd pass wind when I was brushing out his tail. The smell was not pretty, if you get my drift.

Within a year, he was not only well trained but also gentle, with no spook in him. He was ready for me to find him a new home with a loving family. He may never be a great rope horse or a real humdinger of a cow horse, but he was a good all-around using horse. A pleasure to own and ride.

I soon sold him to a young fellow who seemed very excited to buy him. He loaded easily into the excited young fellow's rented stock trailer and except for stepping on my foot again when I was tying him in it, everything went smoothly. I stood on one foot and waved the other one in the air trying to kill the pain while we shook hands and promised to keep in touch. Socks had found his new home.

Within a month the fellow phoned me up. Yes, Socks was a nice horse. Yes, he liked Socks. But, he had found a motorcycle for a really good price and had put a down payment on it. Now he needed to sell Socks in a hurry, to get the rest of the money for the motorcycle. Could I possibly buy Socks back? Being the nice person that I am, I of course said, "No!"

The young fellow developed a slight whine to his voice, and said he would throw in the saddle, blanket, bridle, and the leftover square bales he had bought for Socks — all for the same price he had paid for him. Now, I was willing to deal.

When the young man pulled the horse trailer into my driveway, he was excited about making it to the "two-wheeler dealer" before closing time to pay for his new toy. I opened the end gate of the trailer and Socks nickered a welcome. I untied him and let him step out of the trailer, careful to keep my feet out of the way. He was fat and sassy, with no blemishes. Everything was fine.

It looked like there were at least 20 square bales of hay in the front compartment of the trailer, which I knew would come in handy. I barely had time to glimpse the saddle stuffed up on top of the stacked hay, when the budding biker dude danced in front of me needing his money to get to that dealership in time. I unloaded everything on the double, before handing him his money. He twirled in mid-air and flew down my driveway, tires squealing.

A more thorough inspection of the gear brought disappointment. The bridle was one of those old, wide leather-cheeked ones, with a rusted bit attached to it, worth about $5 if I could find someone to buy it. The saddle blanket had been left somewhere for mice to chew, but would do for a blanket in the corner of the barn for the cats to sleep on. The saddle was ancient — the leather was dried out from never being cared for, the cinch was toast, and the stirrups were missing. I wondered how much Socks was ridden, if his owner used a saddle with no stirrups. At least I got 20 bales of hay out of the deal. The next morning when I cracked open one of those puppies, I discovered it was mildew and mould from one end to the other. It was bonfire time!

Socks settled right in as if he had never left the place. I assured him he was not going to be around long. I took a quick spin on him, and he was as good as gold except for jarring my teeth when he decided to jump a 2-foot-long twig lying on the ground. I figure he cleared that monster twig by a good 4 feet.

A couple of weeks later, he loaded into a young couple's trailer without a care in the world. I let the man load him and made a mental note that Socks never even came close to stepping on his foot. The pretty little woman was already happily planning what toys and treats she would buy for her first horse. Socks was about to be spoiled big time.

Two months later, I again got the phone call. Yes, they loved Socks dearly. He was such a sweetie — their pride and joy — but he acted up something awful when she rode him. After falling off him twice, she was afraid to get back on him. Closing my eyes, I asked what Socks was doing. He fussed and reared, bucked, and jumped sideways. This didn't sound like the horse I knew. The husband got on the line and said that since I had a good reputation as an honest horse dealer, he knew I wouldn't mind taking Socks back. I had obviously sold them a horse that wasn't safe for his wife. I liked the good reputation part and the honest part, but I was having a problem with the buying him back part. Nonetheless, I gave in.

Socks pranced out of their trailer as fat as a hog. His eyes were lit up, and he was ready to do the cha-cha-cha. The little lady slipped him a handful of treats, as she produced his feeding schedule. I was still gazing at the list as they drove away. It included all the second-cut alfalfa hay he could eat, 10 pounds of special rolled, steamed oats/corn with molasses for breakfast, and the same again for supper. He liked his treats at noon, especially the sugar-coated ones made with bran. Just before bed, he needed sliced carrots and apples, or he couldn't sleep.

I led Socks down to the back pasture. He danced around, as charged as a highly fed racehorse on the way to the starting gate. I was glad I wasn't trying to ride him as he reared a couple of times and kicked out in sheer joy with his back legs. He was fat and sassy. He was what I call "out of his cotton-picking mind" from an overload of energy-producing grain. I knew that some time out on pasture with nothing but grass to eat would settle him down. And he'd lose that roll of fat around his middle, too.

About three miles up the road lived two little blond girls with their dad. They spent a lot of time at my place on weekends, cleaning a box stall or two in exchange for riding my quiet horses. Socks soon became their favourite mount. Never once did he step on their cute little cowboy boots or even come close to tossing his head around them. I had let them bridle him with close supervision, and he patiently lowered his head way down for them. He even opened his mouth wide for the bit. Shucks, they could brush his tail, and he never passed gas either. In fact, he was ever so careful with his new friends.

The girls worked hard on their father, begging for the right to own Socks. Dad finally relented, and they rode Socks double down the driveway, waving back at me as they headed for home with their new horse. I waved back, secretly praying that I had seen the last of Socks.

He was back three days later, eating grain out of a sack in the back of my truck that he had ripped open with his teeth. He had obviously escaped somehow. Being full-grown, I refused to cry. Cowgirls don't cry!

I was faced with a dilemma. The father was one of the hardest working men I knew. He was raising these two wee ones as a single parent. He was a dairy farmer working long hours on his own. He would likely not even have noticed Socks was gone and even if he had, I doubted he would find the time to come get him. The girls would be in school. Worse, the family had no telephone, so I had no way of letting them know where the horse was. I was in-between horse trailers and using stock racks on the back of my truck. I was not about to load those racks for a horse needing to go only 3 miles. I nabbed Socks, bridled him, and rode him home bareback. Hopefully, the father was around the barns somewhere and could drive me back to my place.

We made good time, and I soon loped into their yard. A quick look around showed the open gate that Socks must have flipped the latch up on and escaped. I put him back in the corral, found some binder-twine and tied the gate shut. The father was nowhere to be found. I started walking home. Surely someone would come along and offer me a ride.

I arrived home with good-sized blisters on both heels from walking so far in riding boots. They were not meant for walking, they were meant for fitting snugly in stirrups.

Socks showed up again the following Monday. I rode him home again bareback wearing my $9 running shoes just in case. When I returned the escapee, the father informed me the girls were fighting over Socks every night after school. I just studied the tips of my running shoes and was thankful the horse hadn't stepped on my feet.

The next week, we went through the same routine, and the father said his daughters were worried that Socks kept running away because he didn't like them. He added that the girls were also upset because Socks refused to travel at anything but a slow walk with them. What a switch from the last owners' complaint!

The next morning when I found Socks adding fertilizer to my lawn, I was thinking about moving right out of the country so Socks couldn't find me. Just then, a beat-up, old truck and trailer rumbled up my driveway. When the driver stopped and got out, I flew into his arms, bouncing off his tremendous belly. We laughed and hugged while I asked, "What in the holy horrors of Hell are you doing here in this part of the country?" The old boy burped and belched a couple of times and happily informed me that he was looking for a place to rest up for a couple of days. Maybe do some work on his truck. I'm thinking he needs a lot of work on his truck, but I keep that to myself.

Now, this old sport is one of my heroes. He has seen more horses come and go than a dog has fleas. Yup, he's an old-time horse dealer from way back. He taught me that the customer always comes first. While you gotta make a profit, don't be lying to people. Those same people will come back and buy another horse from you years later, if you treat them right. Those same people will give your name to other potential customers, if you're honest. If you're not, they will give you a lot of other names besides the one you answer to.

In his trailer he had two of the cutest bay geldings I have ever seen. Just little guys, about 14 hands high. We chatted about them as we put them in the corral. Jimmy and Jolly had a bit of age on them, but they were real sweetheart kids' ponies. He had picked them up dirt cheap at an estate sale a couple of hundred miles back down the highway.

On the way into the house, we passed Socks nibbling on my kitchen windowsill. I managed to keep from cursing and explained my problem.

The next day, when the girls and their father came to get Socks, they fell in love with the matching bays. It was a match made in heaven — a horse for each of them that would be happy to stay put on their father's farm. My friend was happy with the straight across trade, and I was rid of Socks once and for all. Now if I could just get over missing him, I'd be fine.

Chapter 3
Herman

Back in the good old days, I began my career hauling horses with home-built stock racks on the back of an ancient 1957 Fargo. That truck and I were both stout, stocky, and built low to the ground. Neither of us was known for a whole lot of speed, but put us in mud up to our kneecaps and we could chug through it. We were both known to be hard to get started in the morning, but once going, we could go all day and night with just a shot of fuel every few hours.

When the day came to upgrade to my very first two-horse trailer with matching truck, things took a drastic turn for the worse. The horses that had always loaded so easily in open stock racks didn't take kindly to narrow, enclosed two-horse trailers. Some of my older saddle horses either refused to load or put up such a fight that I was late getting to where I was going most of the time. I figured either I had to go back to using the stock racks or buy new saddle horses.

The new horses weren't much better. The ones that really irked me were the horses that loaded fine on the outward journey, but then wouldn't load to come home again. I missed a lot of suppers because of that narrow horse trailer. Eventually, I figured I was going to have to go back to the "pain-in-the-butt-to-get-on-the-truck" stock racks, or upgrade to a bigger trailer.

The bank lent me the money and I came home with my new stock trailer. Now I could haul four full-sized horses or six little guys, and the horses loved the wide-open back of it.

With the ability to haul so many horses on one trip, I figured I should upgrade my horse operation and start buying and selling more horses. Maybe I could even go into raising the varmints on a bigger scale, besides I needed to turn over more horses to make my monthly trailer payments.

The bank manager frowned a little more than the last time, but finally coughed up a livestock loan so I could increase my number of horses. I was in heaven. This cowgirl was going into big time horse ranching. I would no longer have to work a job in town or ride for some other guy to make ends meet; now I could just hit the road buying and selling, while also increasing my broodmare band numbers.

While I was busy expanding my business, my husband

was getting cranky over me not having time to cook and clean anymore. The divorce wasn't a particularly nasty one. He got the farm and I got the stock trailer, the truck, and the horses. But I had to sell most of the horses to pay off my bank loans, and I needed to buy a new truck to replace the dud that I was driving.

And that's how I met Herman. I fell in love with him the first time I saw him 20 years ago. He was something to see when he was young, and he's still going strong to this day. Herman is a blue 1983 F150 4 x 4 Explorer with a strip of white down his side, and he's still my all-time favourite travelling companion. It's the longest lasting relationship I've had in my life. Herman and I have had some interesting experiences hauling horses together.

One time we headed out on a 16-hour round trip to deliver a horse to the racetrack. I had loaded a gelding to keep the nervous race mare company, and I had also loaded a friend into Herman's cab, to keep me from being too nervous about sending my mare to another person to finish training and race.

We delivered the racehorse and were on our way home. I was getting tired.My friend had never pulled a stock trailer in her life, especially not one with a horse loose in it, but I tried to talk her into driving for a couple of hours. A nervous Nellie, her biggest concern was what if a deer jumps out on the road?

"There are only two things you have to remember,"

I said. "First, you don't worry about the first deer you see crossing the road in your headlights, because it will continue across. It's the deer probably following it that you don't want to hit. Second, you have a live animal back there in that stock trailer, so don't lock your breaks up tight or you will knock the hell out of it. The horse is going to get hurt if it's slammed around in that trailer."

She was not convinced, but I couldn't finish a 16-hour drive. Right about the time I started yammering at her again, the first mule deer appeared in my headlights. True to form, the deer paused only for a second and continued across. As I predicted, the second one appeared from the ditch. I let off the gas and started breaking gently. The second deer continued across. The third appeared, making a mad dash to follow the others. Well, I didn't lock the brakes up real tight, to protect the loose horse in the back, but Herman tried to kiss that deer's rear end before coming to a full stop.

Right then, my nervous friend refused to drive at all. I cranked Herman's radio up full blast, rolled down the window and started singing to keep myself awake. My friend claims she sustained ear damage from the radio and a long-lasting headache from my singing.

It was about a year before I convinced her to come on another horse hauling expedition. This time we were heading out to buy some mares. In the wee hours of the morning, I backed Herman up to the trailer hitch. My friend dropped the ball into place while I dozed in the cab. She quickly went to the house for the thermos of coffee and snacks, while I did my usual trailer check. Hitch done up, safety chains done up, lights working, breaks working. The usual. I thought I had everything in order before climbing back into the truck for 30 more seconds of snooze time.

We were barrelling down the highway at pretty much warp speed since the trailer was empty, there was no other traffic, and Herman was feeling his oats. I was driving with one hand, and had a cup of coffee in the other. My friend munched on a banana for breakfast. Suddenly, with a violent jerk, Herman was thrown to the right. Then Herman was thrown to the left. In my usual calm way, I held my coffee cup out to my friend, "Hold my coffee, please. I think Herman blew a rear tire or something." She reached out and took my cup. Even with my two hands on the steering wheel, Herman leapt sideways.

Then for a split second, everything seemed to be under control, as we both watched a stock trailer much like ours sail past us on the passenger's side. I calmly said, "Boy that trailer looks a lot like mine."

My friend responded by throwing her hands up and screeching, "You idiot, that is your trailer!" as the trailer in question cratered in the ditch.

After that episode, Herman needed repairs to his rear end. The safety chains had destroyed the back of the truck when the trailer jumped off the ball, because it wasn't closed properly. I was just mad about the coffee and banana dripping down off the roof of the cab. The rest was fixable, but those stains are still there. What on earth was she thinking when she threw her hands up in the air like that?

Chapter 4
Lost Trust

What would it be like to lose all trust in others? What if you lost all capacity to care? To feel anything? What if you just gave up? That is what it was like for the old gelding. He was brought down so low by human hands, that he lost the ability to trust, care, or feel.

I didn't want to buy him. It was just one of those things that happens. I had made the long drive to a working cattle ranch to buy a registered quarter horse mare that was advertised for sale.

Like many such ranches, each and every animal must earn its keep in order to stay there. The mare had been one of their better cattle horses for a few years, but after tangling with a barbed wired fence, she became too crippled for riding. Always on the lookout for good broodmare prospects, I had been happy to find her quality bloodlines offered at a very reasonable price. Although not sound for riding, she'd be fine raising colts.

The ranch buildings were set back about a half mile off the main gravel road. As I ambled the old truck and trailer down the lane, I admired the black-and-white cows and their chubby calves grazing the pasture to my left. A hayfield to my right lay newly mowed, drying in the sun. I inhaled deeply to capture the smell of newly cut hay wafting into the truck cab through the open windows.

As I approached the house and yard, I noticed a half dozen saddle horses grazing in a smaller pasture, fat and content with life.

The rancher met me with a smile on his sun-crinkled face, a trusty, old red handkerchief hanging out of his back pocket. In a deep voice he asked, "You the girl come to look at the mare?" I nodded and he continued, "You don't look old enough to be raising horses." Now I grinned too. I was well into my 20s at the time, and he thought I was still just a girl. Shucks, he had just made a friend for life.

Two horses lounged in their corral in the shade of the big, red, hip-roof barn. The man passed the sorrel gelding without a glance, heading towards the mare. As I went past, I did a quick appraisal on the gelding. He was up there in age, with lots of old saddle sores from an ill-fitting saddle. He'd seen lots of feed but was not overly fat; his legs were clean of any serious blemishes. He had a roughly done brand on his hip, and although his head wasn't real pretty, it wasn't bad either. But when I looked into his eyes, I was startled. They were lifeless — totally devoid of anything. To me, a horse's eyes tell a million tales. They can show kindness, bad temperament, concern, fear, love, intelligence, or lack of it. But his eyes were blank slates. He didn't even acknowledge my presence, as his head remained lowered and motionless.

"Just a plug," said the man. I turned my attention to the mare and immediately liked what I saw. She was a stout mare with good withers; all-around good quarter horse conformation. Her pretty head had appealing eyes. Only her legs showed why so many horsemen dread that ripping death called barbed wire. Any horse that gets tangled in it and fights to free herself, will be left with serious scars. The mare was no exception. A slight limp on the left hind leg showed why she was no longer capable of being a saddle horse.

I ran my hands over her, starting on the left side. She tensed for a second as I examined her legs, then she relaxed. Moving around behind her, I found her to be straight legged, with no conformation faults in the hind end at all. As I moved up on the right side of her, I came within touching distance of the gelding. Impulsively, I reached out and stroked his nose. He never moved a muscle; he didn't even blink; yet I had given no warning that I was about to touch him. He should have raised his head, taken a step back, or otherwise reacted to my reaching out towards his face without warning.

Intrigued at this behaviour, I asked, "What is with this horse? It's as if he died, but forgot to fall down." And so I heard the story of Prince, the name I chose for him.

The rancher who now owned him was the proud grand-pappy of a young boy who lived just up the road a piece. The rancher and his son worked the ranch together, the pair of them riding fence lines, doctoring cattle, rounding them up, and in the spring, calving them out. Since his grandson was old enough to sit on the back of a horse (about three years old, he proudly informed me), he and his trusty pony come with them on the shorter day rides. Now the boy's legs had grown too long for the pony, so Grandpappy decided to buy him his own full-sized horse. The horses they already owned were just a hair too much for the little fellow to handle yet.

One Friday he decided to attend a horse sale a couple of hours from home. Arriving at the auction, he toured the pens out back, searching for just the right horse. Like most small town auction sales, the pens were filled with basically undesirable horses. Most were untrained or poorly training at best; several had obvious soundness problems — the old and the just plain unwanted.

Then he spied the sorrel gelding. Saddled and bridled, ready for the ring, the horse stood quietly and patiently. A rather loud man was busy pointing out all the good things about the gelding to another potential buyer. The horse was the best. The quietest. Never bucked, never shied. You could ride him all day and all night and he would never quit on you. This gelding was the best kid's horse he had ever owned.

Now the rancher had been around a few years and was not fooled by all the promises. After all, if the gelding was that great, why was he at a small town monthly auction sale? Prices were always less at these sales than what a man could get for a good horse right at home in his own yard. Something was not being told by the loud, obnoxious man.

After the sale had started, the rancher quietly left the side of the ring to take another look at the gelding. Finding the gelding's pen vacant of the owner, he gave the horse a quick check for soundness. It appeared to be sound in every way. Raising the horse's head, he looked at its teeth to check its age. The horse was around 15 years old. Still, a 15- or 16-year-old horse was okay for his grandson, since the boy would not be riding and working him hard. At least the horse was super quiet, so he wouldn't have to worry about the boy getting hurt.

Later when the gelding and his rider entered the sale ring, the rancher spotted right off that the horse did not neck rein very well, nor did he seem to want to move any faster than a slow walk. The owner had to slap him hard with the ends of the reins to get a bit of animated speed out of him. Still, the gelding was sound and he did want a quiet horse for the boy. His was the final bid.

After paying for the horse, he brought his truck and trailer around to the loading area. On the way back to the pens to collect his new purchase, he passed the owner carrying his saddle over one shoulder. Stopping the man, he said, "Before the sale, you mentioned that your gelding was a good children's horse. How old were the kids that were riding this horse, and how much horse experience did they have?"

The seller shrugged, "Young kids, adults, old ladies, city slickers — they all rode this horse, and very few had any horse experience. I run a dude ranch in the foothills. You don't have anything to worry about with that gelding." With that, he shifted the weight of the saddle to his other shoulder and walked away.

While the rancher was telling me this story, I stroked the mare and watched the gelding. Twice a buzzing horsefly attacked him, but he never so much as flinched. He made no attempt to bite it, kick at it, or even switch his tail at this vicious little monster. Yet when the horsefly switched its attack to the mare, she responded like any horse does — with frustration and every attempt to get it off her. What was wrong with this gelding anyway? It was as though he felt nothing, reacted to nothing. I couldn't figure him out.

The man chuckled, "You came to buy the mare, but all you do is stare at that plug. When you pulled in the yard, my missus would have put the coffee on and I'm willing to bet, found us something to snack on too. We best go in and sample whatever she's put out for us."

I soon decided you would have a hard time meeting nicer people than this man and his bubbly wife. The coffee was the real McCoy — brought to a boil on top of the old gas stove in its pot with a blackened bottom from years of use. The cream was thick and rich, and came straight from a four-legged milk machine. The apple pie was to die for, so I wasn't in any hurry to go home. Contentedly, we moved to the veranda to sip another cup of coffee, while I coaxed him into continuing the story of the gelding. From here, I could still watch the horse, and I noticed that since we were no longer in the corral with him, he was fighting off those darn horse-flies like a normal horse. His head had come up a couple of notches, and he looked more alert. It was the strangest transformation.

The rancher continued his story. When he got the sorrel home from the auction, he cleaned him up, trimmed his mane and feet, and called his son to bring the boy for a visit. The youngster stared at his new horse, eyes big with wonder. A full-sized horse all his own. He loved his fat pony, but he imagined a big horse would be even more fun. He pressed his cheek to the gelding's nose as his grandpa made sure the small saddle fit the gelding's back properly. With a bridle in place, he was ready for his first ride on his very own big horse.

The first problem surfaced immediately. He wasn't tall enough to get his foot in the stirrup to pull himself up. A boost from his dad was ever so embarrassing for this young cowboy. With his father on one side of him and Grandpa on the other in case the gelding did something wrong, he clucked to the gelding to move on out. Nothing happened.

He kicked with his little heals, clucked like mad, and the gelding finally shuffled into gear. Around and around the pen they ambled, the gelding never so much as flicking an ear. After Dad and Grandpa made two trips around, they were satisfied that the gelding was indeed gentle, so they leaned against the rails. "Kick him into a trot," called the boy's father.

He tried. He kicked and clucked and shouted, "Giddy up!" But the gelding continued his slow walk. He slapped the horse with the ends of his reins, just like he sometimes had to do with his pony, but the horse plodded on. Disappointment set in pretty quick.

The next day the three of them saddled up to check a distant pasture of cows. They usually travelled at a fast trot or lope to get where they were going in good time. The boy was soon in tears. Kicking, begging, slapping with the reins produced a slow, pathetic trot that had him falling behind the men, who had to stop and wait for him. The gelding refused to turn anywhere, insisting on following right behind the other horses.

He was an unhappy boy by the time they got back to the barnyard. He wanted his jolly, chubby pony that always did what he asked of her. Grandpa didn't blame him in the least.

The rancher saddled up the gelding himself the next day to find out if he was just a plug or simply taught to go slowly with kids on him. Surely he would liven up with an adult giving the directions.

But the rancher was angry, exhausted, and ready to

shoot the gelding by the time he returned home. Only by spurring hard, something he hated doing, could he get any speed out of the plug. It was as if the gelding just didn't care. He refused to put any life into what was being asked of him.

The rancher's son rode the gelding for the next couple of weeks, as the boy didn't want to. It was a constant battle to get the horse to put some energy into what was asked of him. Finally, he told his father to can the horse, as it wasn't worth the effort.

And that was why the gelding was in the corral with the mare now. The meat horse buyer was expected to show up tomorrow or the next day, getting a liner load ready for a trip to the slaughterhouse. The rancher wouldn't make his money back on the gelding, but he wanted him gone from his property. He figured the horse wasn't worth the grass it took to feed him. I decided to take him off his hands.

I loaded the mare in the front compartment of my stock trailer and Prince in the back. I was hoping there really was a "prince of a horse" hidden inside that gelding somewhere.

Since I had never encountered a horse like Prince before, I chose to keep him in a holding area, where I could observe him for awhile in with some young geldings I was training. He acted just like any other horse, as long as I was nowhere near him. He established himself high in the pecking order with the others, quite able to lunge with ears back at any horse that trespassed in his space. He galloped around with them when the wind came up, just like a normal horse.

However, when I approached the pen, he became a motionless, unblinking, unhearing object. He just stood there, with no life in him at all. He never looked at me; he was a statue with head half hanging. He didn't even chew, for Pete's sake, when I was anywhere near him.

He was not a victim of severe abuse, as he did not flee from me, tremble, become tense, or hold his head high in fear. He was sound, and was not in any pain. He was normal in all respects as long as I wasn't near him. I decided he was a nutcase, pure and simple. Strange indeed.

I worked with horses to help make a living and except for the ol' faithfuls, who had been with me for many years, they came and went as soon as they were trained enough to sell. When I started riding Prince, I found the rancher's story to be true to a tee. I tried a soft colt Bosal, in case it was the bit he feared. No change. I tried riding him bareback in case saddles hurt his back. No change. I tried using strong leg pressure, blunt spurs, and tapping him with a whip with a popper on the end so it made more sound than sting. I spanked his butt with the long colt reins, in an attempt to liven him up. No change. And like the rancher and his son, I gave up. He continued to fascinate me, but it was time to find him a new home.

You'd think that he would be easy to sell to a beginner rider who wanted a quiet gelding to learn on, but even though several such buyers came and tried him out, none bonded with his lacklustre, head-hanging you-do-not-exist,

I-do-not-exist approach to life. No one cared to buy him. My intentions had been to pick the perfect new owner for him, perhaps a woman who would love him enough to bring him out of his shell. But winter was fast approaching, and so were the last horse sales of the year. Since I had to buy all my feed, horses that were trained had to go. I kept him until the very last, then hauled him to the local horse sale.

I felt such sadness, I almost hauled him home again. Perhaps I just hadn't tried hard enough to change what was wrong with him. I didn't know who bought him, and I didn't want to know.

The next spring I got a phone call from another horse-man who just wanted to chat about his new colts on the ground. We traded stories back and forth, surprised we hadn't run into each other at any sales last year. But wait, he had seen me ride a sorrel gelding through the ring late last year — the one with a big ugly brand on his hip. Yup, he bet that horse was a real dud. That brand belonged to someone who had destroyed the minds of more than one poor horse in his possession. It had been said, that some never did recover from his inhumane training practices. I hung up the phone shortly afterwards.

My heart had almost stopped on me. I had forgotten about Prince's brand. Now I knew. I knew who that brand belonged to; Prince's soul was laid bare for me to finally see.

This man never beat his horses. No sir, hardly ever had to use a whip or spurs on them. His claim to fame was that he could make a dude string horse out of anything. Yup, those horses towed the line when he threw those dude riders from the city up on them. The horses didn't dare blink, or they were in trouble.

What he did was the cruelest thing imaginable. If a horse acted up when he was training them to saddle, he simply roped its front feet out from under it, tied all four legs together and left it to lie in the hot, scorching sun. Hell, sometimes all night too, if he felt like it. Then afterwards, he kicked the horse until it struggled to its feet, saddled it up, and rode it all day long without food, water, or rest. He swore he rarely had to do it more than once before the horse never did a thing wrong again in its life.

I knew in my heart now, that Prince was one of those horses. I knew this man had done it more than once to what must at first have been a proud, young gelding. My mind now spoke to Prince, as if he stood before me. "How many times did it take until you finally struggled up with half paralyzed limbs to go all day with nothing to slake your thirst or ease your biting hunger, or a chance to rest your weary heart? Until you gave up entirely?"

It was then that I finally cried for Prince. I cried and screamed a silent scream for a sorrel gelding whose very soul had been snuffed from him at the hands of this man. Oh, Prince, you are gone now, but never forgotten.

Chapter 5
What Are Friends For?

W hen you live alone while scratching out a living breeding, training, buying and selling horses like I do, you need support from friends and family, and I thank the good Lord daily for these people in my life. Without them, I would be toast. Trouble is, some of them will tell you that they were almost toasted themselves helping me.

Simone and the Six Pack

Take Simone for instance. A lady from town who always dresses to the Nines. It took a couple of years to get her to leave her fancy duds at home and wear good old farm clothes. For Simone these farm clothes were usually a tank top, shorts, and cute high-heeled city slicker boots. While I was protected from the elements and the horses themselves in blue jeans, long-sleeved shirts, western hat, and sturdy riding boots, she had to develop other ways to protect herself. Sun tanning lotion on one half of her body and bug repellent spray on the other half seemed to do the trick. While my boots protected me from getting a squashed toe from some horse stepping on my foot, Simone relied on her agility learned from many years of dancing to keep her toes safe. If I had to run to or from a horse in the event of a wreck happening, I thundered along as best I could. She skipped gleefully from one event to another.

Simone is French, and while I don't understand a single word of her native tongue, it didn't take long before my horses were all bilingual, which meant they worked better in two languages for her than they did in one for me.

Simone's pride and joy was the cutest little puddle-jumper of a car — white with multi-coloured decals on its sides. We nicknamed it Spot. My pride and joy was my 1450-pound stallion, Three Kits, who stood 16 hands high. His nickname was Skiddor. Skiddor grazed the lawn during summer so that he did not have to be in his paddock all the time. I failed to warn Simone that horses love to drag their teeth down the hoods of vehicles — some sort of addiction to paint, I believe. The day Skiddor left giant teeth marks all over Spot's hood, roof, and trunk, I did pick up a few choice French words.

Then there was the day I tried to get Simone killed, hand breeding a customer's snotty mare to Skiddor. This mare had a nasty temper at the best of times and was pure hell-on-four-legs once she came into heat. She was also a serious and crazed halter puller if tied to a post, so you can see why no other stallion owner had ever successfully got her bred.

I didn't want to breed this mare because of her disposition, but I failed in my feeble attempts to dissuade the owners. I demanded a complete vet check, hoping a reproductive problem would prove her unfit to carry a foal, but everything was fine. I stalled, saying I didn't want this kind of disposition passed on to one of my stallion's foals, in case he got the blame. Fine, they would not register the foal then. Because of her temperament, I demanded additional money to handle her. Done, I received a cheque for the extra money. I figured that I might as well breed her and get it over with.

My breeding corral has a snubbing post in the middle of it, with an attached, 2-inch thick cotton rope tied high and short. When little Miss Cranky came into heat, we went to the snubbing post. She couldn't break the post or pull it out of the ground. She couldn't break the rope or the heavy-duty halter I had on her either. So she would simply throw herself and hang there. Skiddor is a patient stallion and stood dozing while I came to the realization that the angle-of-the-dangle wouldn't work for him with her in that position.

Okay, so tying her up wasn't the answer. Skiddor agreed.

What Are Friends For?

I put him back out on the lawn, turned the mare loose and headed for town. On the way, I picked up Simone whose car was still in the body shop for repairs to the paint work. We made a stop at the vet's for some tranquilizer. For the mare, readers, not Simone. One Labatt's Blue was all that was needed to calm her nerves.

After Little Miss Cranky was tranquilized, I scotch hobbled her left hind leg, which was still on the ground, to protect the stallion who was taught to approach, tease, then mount from that side. Skiddor stood back beside me, waiting for permission to approach his virgin bride. Simone, to the side of the mare, had one hand on the halter and one holding a twitch firmly attached to the mare's nose. We were ready for the fun to begin.

I clucked to Skiddor, permission to approach the mare. He took two steps, while Little Miss Cranky remained totally oblivious to his approach. Not taking any chances, he gently stuck his nose out and nudged her in the flank. There was not even a blink from that mare. Growing bolder, Skiddor blew hard through his nostrils under her flank. One of her ears did jig up and down once, but that was all. I raised my hand that held his lead rope, which was permission to now do his studly duties.

The magnificent stallion rose up into the air, his forelegs circling the mare's body in a tender display of affection. And the chicken poop hit the fan!

With a scream that would have scared off an attacking

51

cougar, Little Miss Cranky exploded. Forget the tranquilizer; forget the twitch; forget the scotch hobble; she was not about to lose her virginity without a fight. She threw her head to the left and Simone lost hold of the twitch on the mare's nose. That twitch pinged off a fence post clear across the corral. One jump and the scotch hobble, which had been placed on loose so the mare could still bear weight on that leg, was the next thing to go. Everything was a blur. Simone fell and the mare lunged over her. Skiddor, still mounted on the mare, refused to leave his intended target. He, too, went over Simone. She managed to roll her body under the fence before I stepped on her. Good thing too, since my sturdy riding boots can hurt.

Simone survived, although it took awhile to calm her down. She found the last five beers from the six pack of Labatt's Blue a great help. And Little Miss Cranky? She gave birth to a pretty chestnut colt the next spring.

Grandma's Little Helper

A charming young fellow named Travis came into my life shortly after his family suffered the devastating loss of their home to fire one Christmas. To add to their distress, the father became deathly ill for a time.

Although I barely knew the family, I invited the young mother out to my place a time or two for coffee and to give her a much-needed shoulder to lean on, should she need one. She always brought her youngest son along — a little gaffer with freckles and a hint of red in his hair. He reminded me of a spunky colt who could use a few scratches behind his ears to show him that life wasn't all bad. Although he didn't think much of me petting him or scratching behind his ears, one Friday afternoon he asked if he could spend that weekend at my place. Before I could respond, his Mom said, "Sure you can, Sweetheart." As I was busy saying "Well, I have to think on that for a minute," he was fetching his backpack from his Mom's truck and before long was firmly settled on my living room couch. He informed me that the couch was his bed from now on, but I could still sit on it if I wanted to.

His Mom headed out to work and I followed her all the way to the truck, hoping to gain some much needed information. What do I feed him? Do I have to leave water out for him 24 hours a day? And the most important one of all — is he housetrained? (I should mention here that I also raise dogs.) She just smiled and told me I would do fine. How can I do fine? I don't know anything about this business of being a mother. Help!

I muttered to myself, "Okay, I can handle this," as the child followed me out to the corrals. I explained to Travis that he is not allowed in the corrals because some of these horses are rank. They are only at my place to be halter broke, a couple of weeks riding put on them or just plain gentled down a bit. Travis sighed and gently informed me that they have horses too, you know. He is not exactly a greenhorn.

By the time I walked around to the gate, he had slipped

through the rails and crawled in with Gypsy, Bell, and Tiffany. These horses were mature mares that didn't like being handled. Gypsy would take a chunk out of you with her teeth, Bell would run you over, and Tiffany would strike or kick you just for the fun of it.

"Stay calm, Gayle, stay calm," I told myself. "Don't frighten the boy or the mares." Then I screamed, "What in tarnation do you think you're doing? Don't you listen to a thing you're told? Get out of there! You're going to get yourself killed!" Travis calmly petted each mare in turn, his voice soft and loving, and they gathered around him like fleas to a dog.

The first weekend he stayed with me, I fretted so much I lost 10 pounds. By the time summer rolled around, I had grey hair and it was thinner on top from me pulling it out. While he grew and thrived out in those horse corrals, I became a nail-biting wreck. Summer meant two months of school holidays and you can guess where he decided to spend those two months. Yup, I was never going to get to sit on that couch in the evenings anymore. At least he was easy to cook for, got his own water, and was housetrained.

Then came the day he looked at me with love in his eyes and asked, "Can I call you Grandma?" Well I was prouder than an old barren mare getting a chance to be related to an awesome weanling colt. So of course I said, "Sure boy, but there ain't going to be no lazy grandsons on this spread. Now, get out there and get them yearlings caught and tied up to be dewormed."

With the patience of a saint, he replied, "They've been tied up for an hour already, Grandma. I did it while you were putting the stallion back in his pen. I also filled in your daily breeding record book for you, while you were talking to that horse buyer on the phone. Then I counted the tubes of wormer for the horses. You're short one for the yearlings, but don't worry, I checked and you did the bay filly just last month so she's okay until we get to town and buy some more. And by the way, Grandma, I checked and wormer is cheaper at the other store this month, so we can save some money by shopping there."

I just snorted, not ready to admit he sure enough was turning out to be a handy kind of boy to have around. With time, the hair might even grow back on the top of my head the way things were going. Never one to admit it, but I was sort of lonely when his parents wanted him home once in awhile in their big, new house.

Travis and I could get in more trouble than a cat cornered by a pack of dogs. One time we were pulling a horse trailer through the centre of Edmonton. I was nervous to begin with, according to my directions, I wasn't even supposed to be in Edmonton. Travis decided that if I quickly turned left at the next intersection, we could pull into that fast food restaurant to fuel ourselves up while we looked at a map. By then he had me pretty much trained to listen to his directions, so I turned left. I soon figured out that all those cars coming at me honking their horns meant I was going the wrong way on a one-way street. Travis informed me in a nice way, that we missed the restaurant, and when he turns 16, I had better let him drive.

Another time, we hauled two horses to the local horse sale. I was selling a real nice, quiet, registered, two-year-old gelding. He was selling a hammer-headed, crooked-legged, pot-bellied, totally hyped-up, brain-dead yearling gelding that his "loving" grandma gave him. My gelding was a sweetheart in the sale ring. His pride and joy went ballistic in the sale ring. His sold for twice as much as mine. Even the crowd loved this boy.

When Travis and I hauled square bales in my old pick-me-up truck, I figured a good load for the old truck was 54 bales. Travis's job was to stack on top of the load, while poor old Grandma huffed and puffed to throw the bales up to him. Then along came Mel, the man who sold me the hay. He thought my horses could sure use more bales than 54. With a grin, the strong, young man effortlessly threw another 18 bales way up there. He would have continued, but I pointed out that the truck tires were now as flat as pancakes.

He waved cheerily and left to get back to haying in another field. Travis suggested tying down the enormous load of hay perched precariously on the back of the truck. I snarled at him, "Just who is the boss here anyway? Get in the truck." At the first little bump, the entire top half of the load toppled onto the road. Travis stacked, and old Grandma threw those suckers back up to him once more. Travis calmly tied down the load of hay just like it should have been in the first place. I leaned my weary old bones against the side of the truck and wondered what I ever did before this boy came along.

Chapter 6
The Power of Love

The bond between a man or woman and a horse that loves them is a tremendous thing to witness. Love can and does heal many wounds of the soul.

I've often had to take employment in towns in order to help feed the horses and pay the bills. In one town where I was managing a hectic business, I often thought how much easier animals were to deal with than staff and customers. Nonetheless, all my staff were welcome at the farm my husband and I owned, so they could know the pleasure of being around animals. Sundays the business was closed and one wee girl in her early twenties (I'll call her Cindy), used to come out and spend time just hanging around the horses.

Others came to eat, drink, and be merry.

Cindy was a bit of a problem at work. Some days, she was jovial and put the other staff to shame with her ability to outwork them with a smile on her face. Other days, she would be sullen and quiet, seeming not to care about anything. I usually could talk the staff members into giving her a break, but customers were a different matter. I feared that I was going to have to dismiss her, yet I knew in my heart that she would be devastated at being fired. Cindy, I felt, just needed someone to help her along the often uphill path of life.

Slowly her story unfolded, while sitting around the firepit in the growing darkness of a summer's evening.

Raised in a hectic home, she was a forgotten item, treated like nothing more than a mistake that happened. No wonder she suffered from low self esteem. As soon as possible, she quit high school and ventured out into an often cruel world. There she met a countryman who introduced her to horses and the power of love. She was happy and content. With horses, she found a shared bond of need and trust. She learned how to handle and care for these four-legged friends. Then came the news. Her man had grown tired of her. She was shattered. As she told us this story, Cindy's sobs brought tears to my husband's eyes as well as my own.

Then began her life of drinking and mind-destroying drugs. This was the girl who now worked for me. Some days she could cope with life; many days she could not.

Out in my corrals stood a wreck of a yearling. I had

bought a bred mare to add to my broodmare band, and she foaled a grade colt, as homely as sin with twisted front legs. I had yet to sell him, even though I knew he was only good for slaughter. No one was going to buy this wreck of a colt. I trimmed his feet religiously, trying to straighten his front legs. I paid to geld him. I hoped he would grow into a head that was two sizes too big for the rest of his body. But that was never going to happen.

It was this horse Cindy was drawn to. They formed a special bond. He romped with her as if she was another colt his own age. They spun circles and frolicked together; they played games of tag. I had never bothered to name him, so she promptly named him Jumper even though with his deformed front legs he couldn't jump a mud puddle.

Finally, the time came when I had to sit her down in my office and explain that even though I thought the world of her, I was going to have to dismiss her because of her moodiness and complaints from customers and other staff members. I recommended she get counselling for the issues that were troubling her. I also recommended that she look into a different career that would allow her to work with animals, as I felt she had a natural ability to care for them. This was not easy for me, and we both ended up crying. When she stood to leave my office, she said in a small, timid, yet clear voice, "Don't sell Jumper; I'll be back to buy him." She walked out. I sniffled. Then I straightened in my chair, once again the Boss Lady I was paid to be.

Jumper wasn't any better looking as a two year old. Both his front legs still toed out so badly, he was unfit for anything except perhaps being trail ridden in a straight line. I didn't even take the time to start him under saddle. Yet, I still hadn't hauled him to an auction mart to watch him go for meat either.

Then, one day Cindy phoned me at work. She apologized for bothering me, but did I still have Jumper? She was trying her best to get her life back on track. In fact, her grandma was paying for a therapist to help her deal with her problems. She was working again but part-time, as she still had a lot of problems relating to other people. She was now renting a home in the country with a couple of other young people. Together they had several dogs, cats, and even some chickens. They had good pasture for a horse. The therapist agreed that if she loved horses, she should look into getting one. In fact he thought her heart would heal far more quickly with something of her own to love and care for. How much did I want for Jumper?

I listened quietly as she continued. She was off drugs and rarely went to a bar anymore. She was growing up. She still had a long road ahead of her, and she knew that, but perhaps Jumper would help her along the way. She remembered clearly every second she had spent with him. She had even found someone to help her train him. She felt sure that together she and Jumper could conquer the world.

I gave her Jumper. No money changed hands. I

delivered him to her place and watched her face light up with such radiance, when he stepped out of the trailer.

The rest is a fairy tale come true. Cindy told me that it was Jumper who finally broke through the ties binding her heart. He gave her unconditional love and never judged her when she made mistakes. When she needed a friend to talk to, Jumper listened, often deep into the night, rubbing his head on her chest while her arms were wrapped around his neck. Even as I write this, Cindy still owns Jumper. He is very old now and arthritis has affected his front legs, but the pair of them still go for short trail rides now and then on his 'feeling good' days.

The crooked legged horse that I almost sold for meat so very many years ago will draw his last breath on her and her family's land when the time is right. Cindy, her husband, and children will mourn his passing.

Chapter 7
The Mare Who Got into the Whisky Barrel

In the olden days, I had a four-year-old, first-time foaling mare. She foaled with one mighty small udder for such a big, well-fed mare. Sure, the filly was getting some much-needed colostrum, but nowhere near enough milk to survive. By eight hours old, she had resorted to sucking the few drops of milk from her dam, then burying her tiny muzzle in the water tank and gulping down water. Desperate, I phoned the old-time vet who was the only one in the area. He didn't know of any shots at that time to give a mare to increase her milk supply. But he did have the oddest thing for me to try. He claimed it would work within hours.

He told me to phone the nearest distillery that made whisky. Apparently, after the whisky is siphoned off for us to guzzle, a sludge is left in the bottom of the wooden barrel. The distilleries dry the sludge into a powder which is used for medicinal purposes (just animals I hope) and for fertilizer to grow super-sized plants. (I have no idea if these super-sized plants lean slightly to the side or sway even when there is no breeze.)

I ordered a 5-pound bag of this dried whisky mash, which they put on the midnight express bus to my town. When I went to the bus terminal to pick it up, the lady handed me the package with her nose all wrinkled up. It wasn't my horsy smell bothering her, but the smell coming from inside the brown paper wrapping. It was so bad, I transported it home in the back of the truck, not inside the cab with me.

I mixed a hefty dose of the powder in the mare's morning grain. She took to the taste of it like an old drunk who's been deprived for quite a spell. She had another feeding in the afternoon, then again at night. By the next morning's feeding that mare was hooked on the stuff. She wasn't leaning sideways or tripping over her own feet, but I swear she had a glazed look in her eyes. By nighttime, she was milking like a Holstein cow, and the little filly was in seventh heaven.

Strange as it was, this old-time remedy worked. The filly couldn't consume all that available milk, and the mare eventually got over her need for her three-times-a-day fix of leftover whisky.

Chapter 8
Stormy's Donkeys

This book on horses would not be complete without a tale about the charming donkey, relative to the horse. My dear friend, Stormy O'Shea, an avid donkey fan who keeps some of the little critters around just for amusement sake, has had some fun times with her donks. Here's what she has to say.

All the books say a donkey is just like a horse. They are part of the equine family. Whoever wrote those words of wisdom should have interviewed my small herd of donkeys. They would have brayed stridently that they certainly were not just like a horse, although they do share some similarities. They all have the basic body shape, except for those beautiful long ears on the donks. They eat hay and oats, and graze on lush grass. Most have a love of carrots, apples, and specially made horse treats. However, being owned by several donkeys, I know they are miles apart from horses.

You can put most horses in a corral and not worry too much about them being bored. Put several more in, and they will usually stand around waiting patiently to be fed or let out. Not so with donks. They will constantly circle the pen, looking for anything to snack on, nibble at, chew to bits, or push out of shape.

Donkey Games

I was in my garden one afternoon, when a pickup came flying up the driveway. Two rugged cowboys spilled out whooping with laughter. I called out a greeting but all they could do was point out to the pasture, tears of laughter streaming down their cheeks. I knew immediately that my donks were up to something. Sure enough, they were.

Two of them had found an old white feed sack. With their teeth firmly clamped one on each end they were racing madly in a circle, much like two children holding hands and spinning. As we watched, one let go and the other galloped towards a group of young colts sharing the corral. The donkey whacked them with wild enthusiasm on their rear ends with the sack. The poor colts stampeded from pillar to post, with the donk in hot pursuit.

Meanwhile, my husband had come out of the barn to see who had driven up. When he saw the donkeys' antics, he shot me a look that told me I was in big trouble. Not that it worried me much. It was nothing that a juicy steak dinner followed by a thick slice of apple pie couldn't fix. Of course, he wanted me to tell the cowboys what had happened the day before and how one of those darn long eared critters almost caused two old ladies to have heart attacks.

Abby's Cat

Abby is a donkey I rescued, and she had grown into a beauty. I learned early she needed toys to amuse herself. Since I have a bevy of tiny housedogs, I keep a huge box of stuffed animals for them to play with. I chose a realistic looking orange cat that was too big for the small dogs to play with. Out to Abby it went. She was delighted! She immediately grabbed the stuffed thing by the tail, then lit out at full gallop for the pasture. Donkeys are generous, so they like to share new toys. The colts saw her coming and didn't appreciate Abby's enthusiasm. They galloped full steam out to the back forty.

Having no other playmates, she amused herself by swinging the cat by the tail, whipping it in a circle, then letting it fly into the air in a high arc. Once it landed, she would trot over to it, stomp on it a few times, pick it up by the tail and do it all over again. I was bent over double, laughing at her antics, when a car screeched to a stop in the driveway.

Two little grey-haired ladies tumbled out in a dither. "What kind of person are you to allow a donkey to hurt that poor cat? And you're standing here doing nothing?" One lady had a cane, which she pounded on the ground with every word. The yelling continued. "We're going to report you. Just see if we don't. Get out there and rescue that poor cat. It's probably dead! If that sad, mangled thing is still alive, we'll take it straight to the vet."

As I tried to explain, their shrieking drowned me out. Meanwhile Abby was trying something new. She had the cat by the head and was methodically banging it against a fence post. The old ladies were in hysterics by now, jumping up and down in a rage. I wondered if I should offer to make them a nice pot of calming tea.

All the racket caught Abby's attention. Still with the stuffed cat dangling from her teeth, she trotted up to the fence. She dropped the toy and put one foot on it. By this time, the dear ladies were hanging on to each other moaning and sobbing. Abby liked the sound. She sucked in some wind and roared out one good bray after another.

With every bray, the women seemed to shrink in size. I finally reached under the fence and yanked the stuffed cat out, showing them it was just a toy. Not a real cat. I thought they would be relieved and would smile and then apologize for all the nasty things they had said.

Not so. In perfect unison they screeched, "You are sick, sick, sick! What sort of person gives a donkey a thing like that to play with?" There was more thumping with the cane, this time on the hood of the car. Abby liked that sound too, so she continued braying. Anyone who knows donkeys understands what a loud, powerful voice they have. While Abby was enjoying her sing, the ladies who had worked themselves into a fine lather, decided they had had enough of this crazy place. Both women tried to get into the car from the same side. One leaned on the horn. The other used her cane like a cattle prod to hurry her companion into the vehicle. Both were still hollering.

They finally stuffed themselves into the car, rolled down the windows and continued to hurl insults at me. I was impressed. I had no idea that tiny old ladies would have such a wide selection of cuss words.

I didn't give Abby back her stuffed cat. Being a little rattled by the whole scene, I dug out a large cardboard box for her to play with. When I tossed it over the fence to her, she flipped it with a foot. It flew into the air, landing on her head. She thought it was great fun! Abby trotted out to the pasture where the colts were grazing. It was too much for them to handle — a donkey, minus a head, coming right towards them.

I wonder if our colts will some day need psychiatric help for the trauma my donkeys have inflicted on them. More likely they will turn out able to handle anything. As for me, I look forward to each day wondering what new thing my donkeys will come up with, knowing they'll serve up a lot of laughter as good old stress relief.

Chapter 9
A Case of the Strangles

L ife is not always a bed of roses when you're raising horses. There are good times and there are bad. You learn to cope with the challenges anyway you can, and you learn to depend on the veterinarians in your life. Without them, many a horse would be lost.

I had purchased a pretty, grey yearling filly sight unseen and had her delivered to my home. She looked to be in good health when unloaded from the trailer, but I put her in a separate pen away from the others as a safety precaution. The next day she wasn't looking very chipper, and sure enough, she was in the first stage of distemper (strangles), a highly contagious equine disease. And separate pen or not, all my other horses started to get strangles, too.

I have long followed the advice to let strangles run its course unless the animal is desperately ill with it, and none of my horses were so sick that they needed treatment. They were an unhappy bunch with their swollen glands under the jaw, but the glands were draining without assistance.

Only my 20-year-old mare, Lady, showed no signs of having contracted the disease. When I did a final check on the horses just before dark, I found Lady far from the herd, sitting like a dog. She was in terrible distress and the ground around her was torn up from her struggling. Finding a horse in this unnatural position is a desperate situation. I phoned the closest vet to come right away. He diagnosed her quickly. His diagnosis was that she had colicked and had a twisted gut or ruptured bowel. He advised she should be destroyed immediately, as she could not survive this condition.

I was well aware that horses found in this unnatural position usually had a twisted gut or ruptured bowel, but I suggested that she instead might have bastard strangles (when the disease moves from the head to the internal cavity) and that the pain was causing her to adopt the position she was in. The vet repeated his diagnosis and offered to destroy the mare for me or I could shoot her myself. He had no intention of trying to treat a horse already dead on its feet. He is not an unkind man, but he did not want to stand by and watch her suffer.

Old Lady did not deserve to suffer, but she did deserve

further examination before pulling the trigger. I asked the vet to give her a high dose of painkiller and another dose for me to give to her later on the long trip to the university in Saskatoon, the only facility that might be able to save her. He grudgingly agreed. Within minutes, the pain was masked by the drug and she was able to stand. Still, her heart rate was far too high for her to keep going much longer. I loaded her in the trailer and set off down the long, lonely highway.

I cannot say enough about the veterinarian staff at the University of Saskatchewan. After arriving, they quickly confirmed a serious case of bastard strangles. They agreed to try to save her, but did not hold out much hope.

The first task was to get her pulse back down to an acceptable level, and they gave themselves only a couple of hours to do so. They succeeded. It was a lengthy, uphill battle for her life over the next several days. She was kept drugged so she was free of pain. The vets were repeatedly forced to tap into her under-belly, to drain off the pus accumulating inside her. She was administered gallons of fluids by intravenous drip into her jugular, 24 hours a day.

For days they never left her stall, drawing on all their knowledge to save the life of this grand old mare. And she did survive. In fact, although heavily pregnant during this ordeal, miraculously she didn't lose the foal. His name is Zeke and he is a beauty to behold. Had I not insisted on a second opinion so long ago, two horses would have died that day, not just one.

Chapter 10
Cow Tales

E veryone thinks that being a cowgirl out on the open range must be so much fun. And it is, if you like long days, seven days a week. The job has its perks. You get to ride with all those good-looking cowboys, for a start. And if they are the Real McCoy, they even like you with calf manure smeared on your cheeks and sweat stains in the armpits of your shirt. As long as you can hold up your end of the job, they may even give you the occasional compliment. "Hey Blondie, get that nag of yours in high gear or I may have to come over there and slap your little rump."

You say to yourself, "I love this guy already; he thinks my rump is little."

"Hey Blondie, nice job of cutting that lame steer out of the herd. One of these days I'm going to take you to town and buy you a beer." You turn beet red, after all, didn't he just ask you out on a date in cowboy lingo?

"Hey Blondie, I sure hope you can cook as good as you can ride." Oh, my Gawd! I barely know this dude and he wants to marry me. Why else is he wondering if I can cook? I am going to go straight to town to buy some cook books. It's time I learned how to make something besides chili and beans anyway.

Now there is a difference between a real cowgirl working on a big ranch and one who rides horses for pleasure. You know the ones I mean, with the jeans so tight they must be painted on. In the real world, when you are riding horses 10 to 14 hours a day, you don't wear skin-tight jeans. You wear comfortable jeans, so you can get up and down off that horse countless times a day, chase that calf on foot, wrestle bare-handed with the calf's irate mother, and then give a shot of penicillin to that 2000-pound bull with foot rot. You wear pants you can actually run in if you have to.

A Snotty Cow

I was glad I was wearing my comfortable jeans the time I got day work from a rancher helping round up some stray cows on a large grazing lease. It was mostly dense bush, with occasional cattle or game trails and uncooperative cows. We had spilt up, gone to the far reaches of the land and were now pushing strays towards a holding area on the flats along the river.

The strays were small groups of cow/calf pairs that were content living right where they were. None seemed overly enthusiastic about being moved home for the fall and winter.

I was quite happy with the few I had convinced to mosey along, staying well back of them to keep them calm, so they wouldn't get riled up and head in the wrong direction.

Then I spotted a lone Angus cow off to my right. She was standing motionless back in the tree line — head up, watching me but obviously thinking she was hidden. I always had to chuckle over these critters who had grown wild enough during a summer in the high country to think that they now blended into the bush like a deer. Since she was as black as the ace of spades, she didn't blend in at all.

I eased my gelding back, meaning to circle in behind the cow and get her headed out. The trouble is that when I approached her, she did not mosey off in the right direction but instead spun to face me, with her head up in the air. She shook her head, warning me she wasn't interested in cooperating. A quick glance told me she was a dry cow who had lost her calf a long time ago. The good news was that I didn't have to hunt for the calf. The bad news was that sometimes these old single cows with no calf can be harder to convince to join the others.

I slapped my hand on my chaps and hollered for her to move out. She took two steps in my direction, shook her head again and pawed the ground with a front foot, throwing dirt up on her back.

Great. Why did I have to be the one to find some old snotty cow? I hollered again, slapping my leg for more sound effects and jumped my gelding towards her. These three things combined should have worked, and I should have been looking at her back end going away from me. Instead, she lowered her head to the attack position, threw more dirt up on her back and gave me an ear splitting bellow, which in cow language meant "attack mode now on standby."

I hollered again. She bellowed again, and a split second later she charged my horse. She rooted him a good swipe on the left shoulder before I got him turned around in the heavy bush to get out of her way. She then gave him a parting thump in the rear end as we were leaving.

The gelding took everything in stride as if getting hit by a cow was something that happened all the time and was no big deal. I made a mental note to jack the price up on him a bit for having more than his fair share of common sense.

I circled the cow again, making lots of noise in the bush, trying to get her to leave the country. She circled with me, head lowered, ready to fight. So I moved in close, then spun the gelding around, looking back over my shoulder to check that she was hot on his tail. Sure enough, she chased us a good 50 yards, before taking another stand. And that is how I got her down to the bunched cattle along the river. Stop, go back and bug her, have her chase us several yards. Stop and do it over again.

The Heart of a Horse

Several men were lounging around the holding area watching this performance once we hit the open pasture. I realized my method of chasing cows would seem odd to these cowboys. I also realized that since I was the only woman on the roundup, I was likely in for a bit of ribbing. I figured the one I had secretly nicknamed "Backscratcher" due to his three day growth of prickly stubble on his chin would be the worst heckler. Or perhaps "Drugstore Cowboy," the one with the expensive cowboy boots, silver spurs, and bright red bandana tied around his neck. Or maybe it would be "Weasel," the small one with the shifty eyes and quick, jerky movements that even bothered his horse. I prayed that "Handsome Man," the good-looking charmer my age would not be the one to rib me, since I kind of liked the way he filled out his blue jeans. I was secretly hoping to impress him with what a great cowgirl I was.

Dismounting from my horse, I stretched and busied myself with loosening my cinch. Ignoring the men gathered around me, I rubbed my horse's shoulder, letting him know I was pleased with his performance. Much to my chagrin, Handsome Man just couldn't help himself, "You're sort of new at this chasing cows business, aren't you?" he said. "Perhaps I should explain to you that you chase cows from behind them, not in front of them." At this, the rest of the men exploded in loud guffaws, thinking Handsome Man was the smartest thing since sliced bread.

Slowly I turned towards my tormentor, trying to think of

78

an appropriate and lady-like comeback. I was prepared to bat my eyelashes if necessary. But I didn't have to because just then I noticed that he had tiny hairs growing out of his nostrils and I just don't like a man sporting nose hair, no matter how he fills out his blue jeans!

Scared Stiff

Not all horses stay calm and controllable after getting kicked by a cow. In fact, over the years I learnt that some react in a completely unpredictable way.

I did a fair amount of riding on a neighbour's ranch since I lived on a small acreage. In return for letting me mile out horses on his land, I kept an eye on his cattle for him. Most of his bottomland was cleared and planted to pasture, but there was plenty of bush and timber remaining higher up the slopes. It was a pleasant place to ride.

I had several weeks' riding on a three-year-old gelding and although he had a bit of spook in him, he was a nice horse. While trotting down a cut line on him, I came across a mother cow in the bush. I could see her calf lying on the ground beside her. The calf was not lying up on his chest in a healthy position, but flat on the ground, head thrown back. From the position he was in, I figured him to be dead and past any help from me. But unless I got close enough to see if he was breathing or not, I couldn't know for sure.

I moved quietly towards the cow, so she wouldn't think she had to get into 'protect my calf' mode. I circled her, coming in even closer, but still I could not figure out if the calf was breathing. The cow shook her head at me, blowing drops from her nose. I sure didn't want to tangle with an irate mother cow, but I still couldn't see the calf well enough. Now, any old cowman will tell you, "Keep the calf between you and the cow to prevent getting hit." I followed this advice and eased the already tense gelding towards the calf, with Momma on guard duty on the other side of it.

At about the same time that I saw that the calf was indeed no longer in the world of the living, Momma cow decided to put the run on me. She dropped her head and charged. I was too close to get out of her way in the thicket of small trees. She hooked my horse in the cinch area, and I got ready for the wreck to happen. This green-broke gelding was about to blow, and I just hoped I could stay with him.

Instead, he froze. She hooked him under the belly again, just missing my leg by inches. She then hammered him in the hind leg. The silly horse just took the beating, making no attempt to get away. Frantic, I spanked his butt with the reins, and I swear he rooted himself more firmly to the spot.

The old cow made one more pass at him then turned tail. She had made her final stand to protect her dead offspring.

I knew I was in bigger trouble now than if the horse had blown up and taken off running and bucking. He was trembling violently and his mind was shot. He wasn't able to rationalize what had just happened or to figure out that the danger was over. He had me plumb spooked, because I knew I didn't want to be anywhere near him, let alone on him, when he finally decided to move.

I stepped off him slowly and gently, and inched as far from him as I could while still holding onto the reins. I moved towards his rear and pulled on the rein to untrack him and get him to move.

He moved all right. He shot straight in the air, came down, reared and flipped right over backwards. He lunged back to his feet and then his ears started to rotate — a positive sign that he was able to think again.

I had let go of the reins when he came unglued. Talking quietly to him, I picked up his reins again. I pulled on his head again, and he followed the pull without exploding. I led him around a bit, until he was almost back to normal. He was not seriously injured physically, so I approached him to mount. The old cow had hammered him on his left side. I reached towards the stirrup and he started to kick. He just stood there and kicked with that hind leg. Wham, wham, wham. Okay, I would just have to mount him from the right side. I moved around to that side, reached for the stirrup and he switched kickers just as quick. He didn't do anything else; he just stood there and kicked.

I headed for home, leading him. Every once in awhile he would kick straight out behind. After about a mile, I was able to mount in between the now sporadic kicks.

He kicked on and off all the way home. I turned him out

for a couple of weeks, and he was fine after that. But I sure didn't check cows on him again.

Chapter 11
Old Flip

love listening to my 82-year-old mother, Becky Caskey, tell stories about when she was a young girl. Born in Alberta in 1921, she grew up when horses worked the land and pulled the buggies to town. Granddad and his brother grew tall, yellow crops of grain, raised some of the best purebred horned Hereford cattle, and never lacked for horse power.

Their teams came in all sizes, ages, and colours. In those days, horses were not pets; they worked for their hay and oats. They were well cared for, but until age brought them down, they leaned into their collars, straining to haul their loads. And the horses loved it. Many a horse was disgusted to be left behind when the workday began at morning light, and showed it by nickering and dancing to go too. They were bred to work, and the best of them are fondly remembered to this day.

Mom has told me many amusing and touching stories of the special horses in her life — Blazer, Beauty, Star Lion, Judy, and a team of bay Hamiltonians named Buster and Barney.

Mom raised the orphan colt, Blazer, by hand. The colt still loved drinking milk from an old mixing bowl even when he was two years old. He would paw at an old log outside the house to summon mother for his milk. He pawed a hole almost right through the log before finally giving up his addiction.

Mom brought another favourite horse of hers, named Beauty, into the house porch one time just to see if she could. Grandma tried chasing them out by whacking them both with a straw broom. Poor Mom was squashed against the porch wall by the panicked horse trying to turn around in the confined space to get away from that broom.

Mom also tells the tragic story of Uncle's favourite mare, called Judy, who shared a soul-deep bond with him. One day she tripped in a badger hole. Uncle was thrown and broke his leg. A neighbour saw the horse standing there and went to investigate. Judy refused to let this stranger near her fallen rider, whirling around Uncle in protective anger to keep the man away. He was forced to walk a long way to fetch Granddad. Then came the sad day Judy refused to leave the corral when asked to. Uncle picked up a small stone and winged it at her to get her to move. Such a tiny stone, but it struck her on the front leg, shattering the bone.

Uncle in his grief and despair, had to shoot his beloved mare. He skinned her, tanned the hide and slept with this horsehide blanket for the rest of his life. I now own this blanket. Although it is well over 70 years old, it remains one of my most prized possessions.

But there is one horse from my mother's past that stands out above all the rest — Old Flip.

Flip was raised in the Oyen, Alberta area. While still a wee foal, her mother was put to work doing road construction. Running beside her sweating mother, Flip soon became quick and agile, as she leapt aside out of harm's way, hurdled over banks of dirt, and turned on a dime to avoid collisions with men and other teams bent to the task at hand.

One day when she was older, a neighbour's big breeding bull escaped from its pasture. Three horsemen were summoned to get him back in. Soon the bull was plumb riled up and in a murderous temper. It hooked the underbelly of one of the horses, tossing the horse and its rider over backwards. Flip, being ridden by another man, proved her quickness and ability to handle the snorty old bull. She whirled in behind the bull and bit his rump, sinking her teeth into him again and again. The bull was fast and kept whirling to hook her. But Flip was faster, spinning around and around with him, with her snapping jaws repeatedly finding their target.

Finally the defeated bull headed for his home range. He had had enough of the demon horse.

Flip was built much like today's popular breed of horse — the quarter horse. She could turn on a dime and give you a nickel in change. When you said, "Whoa," she stopped dead in her tracks, and you better be prepared for it or be flung over her head.

Mom was almost eight years old, when Uncle bought Flip. She stood in awe as he led her up the lane. Wow, her very own school horse. She was a sharp-looking bay mare with a squiggly white blaze on her forehead. They became friends right away. Flip trusted Mom, and Mom loved her. They were meant for each other.

Flip was head shy and hated anyone touching her face. It wasn't clear what her second owner, an often cruel horseman, had done to her. What Mom did know was that her tongue had been almost cut in half. A deep scarred groove remained. Flip was a confirmed halter puller, freaking out if tied by the halter on her head. She would pull and fight being tied until every single rope broke. What was Mom going to do? Well, she tied her up by her front foot, which Flip never minded in the least. Granddad put a small leather strap with a buckle onto a short piece of rope for Mom. Flip would lift her foot up, so Mom could buckle it around her pastern, then stand patiently while tied up at home, at the school house, church, or anywhere.

Mom didn't ride Flip often. She couldn't stay on a horse

and no one could figure out why. After all, her brother had been riding since he was five years old. He was an excellent rider. Mom simply fell off every time she got on a horse; that was all there was to it. She loved horses and had no fear of them whatsoever, but falling onto hard ground again and again was no fun. Instead, she hitched Flip to a buggy and went to school that way. She never had to pick up the shafts of the buggy for Flip; Flip would just back straight in for her. But if anyone else tried to do it, Flip would back crooked and straddle first one shaft, then the other.

The buggy worked wonders for her, until winter set in. Now what were Granddad and Uncle going to do so she could make the 14-mile round trip, to school? They did not own a cutter for a single horse. This was the late 1920s, a time of little money but great pioneer spirit and resourcefulness. A homemade toboggan was fashioned from an old binder platform. Mom's brother made a hood for it like the one found on a baby's buggy. Shafts for Flip were added, and Mom's very own "bumperett" was born. It didn't have a seat in it, so Mom sat on a tanned sheepskin on the floor. Heavy rugs kept her warm. As time went on, the bottom of the bumperett began to wear thin so runners were attached to the base. This was Mom's winter conveyance for all of her school years.

Flip did not like other horses to pass her. One cold winter morning on the way to school, Flip had broken trail through the deep fresh snow, when someone with a team decided to pass them. She was pretty upset about that. Then a boy on a young black mare galloped past. This was just too much of an insult for Flip. She decided to gallop also. Going around a bend in the road, the bumperett ticked her heels, and she was off like a shot. First, she passed the team like they were standing still. Then she shot past that boy on the galloping mare, showing him how fast a real racehorse could run. This was a lot of fun, until Mom realized they were completely out of control and headed straight towards the school's barn doors. She thought a terrible wreck was about to happen, but Flip came to a screeching halt just in time. Unfortunately, when they came to a standstill, the bumperett was perched on top of a snow bank and Flip was below on the path, which made it a challenge to unhitch her.

The last winter that Mom went to the little white schoolhouse on the prairies, the temperature hovered around –37° Celsius all of January and right into February. The blizzards started most afternoons. Grandpa had always told her that if she was caught in a blizzard, to let the horse go where it wanted to. A horse's sense of direction is far better than a human's.

Well let me tell you, the first thing that happens in a blizzard is that your trail vanishes under drifting, blowing snow. In the whiteout, Flip and Mom got to the last long hill, and then lost the trail. Mom remembered what Grandpa had told her and gave Flip her head, trusting her to get them home safely. Flip ploughed ahead, her face bent into the wind. After what seemed like forever, she came to a halt. No matter how Mom urged her to get going again, she refused to move. When Mom got out and walked around in front of Flip to investigate, she found flimsy square boards sticking up out of a snow bank. Now she knew where they were! She and Flip had drifted to the southeast of the yard, and those boards were part of the roof of the root cellar that Grandpa had dug into the side of a sandy hill. Below those flimsy boards was a deep pit. Had Flip taken another step, they would have crashed through and perished. They never would have been found in blizzard conditions so far off the trail.

Growing up on a lonely prairie farm, Mom had no one to tell all her worldly troubles to. No one but Flip. Many a time, when Mom was sad about something and needed a friend, she would talk to Flip. Flip would nudge her with her nose, then she would lay her old head on Mom's shoulder and close her eyes. They would stand like that, a girl and her horse.

There was not a lot of feed in the Dirty Thirties and Forties, and farmers struggled just to feed their cattle. In winter, all horses were turned out on the prairie to paw for feed off the land. Only a team and one good saddle horse were kept in the barn for the winter months. When Flip was 32 years old, Mom begged her dad to let the old mare stay home for the winter, but her pleas fell on deaf ears. Feed was just too precious.

Flip managed to make it home in the early spring. She was terribly thin with such sunken eyes. She walked up to the old barn doors and lay down, never to rise again. Mom felt such terrible grief. Old Flip, not just a horse, but a dear friend.

Chapter 12
Lights Out!

hrough years of raising, training, and buy-
ing and selling horses, I've learned a lot of
things. I've learned that if you raise horses
right, they are much easier to train than the ones you
purchase from auction sales. Horses from auctions have
often been spoiled rotten or they've been scared spitless by
someone mishandling them. You have to work to remedy
these things in order to make good horses out of them.

Buying them off the open range was a common practice
of mine in the 1970s. I only had to outbid the meat horse buyers to get the majority of these wild-eyed critters. Back in
those days, they were mostly grade horses of unknown
pedigree, but I would only buy the good looking beggars with

nice conformation. They were often not castrated, had matted manes and tails, and blew snorts of terror through their noses. Half the time they had never seen a man on foot let alone been this close to a whole pack of humans. They had never been fed hay or grain, and had grown up fighting to survive, struggling to find food or shelter. They had learned to flee from predators or to stand and fight. They were tough horses either frightened out of their wits or on the warpath, looking for a fight. I tried to pick out the in-between ones. The ones that were only going to break one or two bones, not outright kill me.

In the good old days, we seldom had round pens or arenas to ride our horses around day in and day out. Instead, we hoped for some old cow corral that was high enough and strong enough to get them halter broke and gelded. Then trainers such as myself worked with them for two or three days, by gently touching them all over with our hands, talking softly to them, earning their trust. We eased in close to lay an old saddle blanket on, over and around them. Most of us never thought of tying plastic bags or other paraphernalia onto long whips to touch them all over in order to stay back and protect ourselves. So we got struck, kicked, or bitten occasionally, but we called it "hands on" training. We never thought of chasing a horse away from us, making him go around and around, until he "joined up" with us by learning that the only place he got to rest was right beside us.

Instead, many of us trainers were proud when we could

say, "Lookie here! He just came to me to be scratched. He trusts me." "Why, the bugger likes me. Look at the way he is following me around!" We never had fancy words for it back then. Phrases such as "joining up" hadn't been invented yet. I know that the broncs came to me because they trusted me, not because the only place that was safe from being chased around a pen was beside me or following me. And I'm not talking about today's average horse that is handled since birth. I'm talking about horses that were semi-wild and real tough from life's hard lessons of survival of the fittest.

After a couple or three days of working with these horses, they were saddled and ridden out on the land, not in the safety of pens or arenas. Some took to the saddle and being ridden like they'd been doing it all their lives. I often put a lot of extra time on these nicer ones. The day I could slide off their rumps, crawl under their bellies, cross a creek or river on them, throw a rope off them, and ride them bareback, they went to good homes. The families would never have guessed their fat, fancy, and trimmed up gelding at one time shivered and shook at the sight of a human.

Some were snotty broncs, and many of them could buck without needing much excuse. A lot of cowboys didn't care though. These horses didn't cost a fortune and they added some excitement to their lives. Old-time cowboys weren't afraid of anything on four legs back then.

One tough horse I thought the world of was a grade black gelding I purchased from a stock contractor. He had been used as a bareback bronc and never did learn to like being a saddle horse. But I just had to have him, because I needed a black horse to get married on. That's a pretty good reason for this cowgirl.

I survived the wedding on him and went on to continually place in the top four in competitive trail riding. Twenty-five milers, 50 milers, Son didn't care. I gave him a job to do and he did it. All he asked was that I allow him his self-respect and didn't pet him too much or too long when the awards were handed out. He never did learn to appreciate that human/horse bonding thing, after his stint as a rodeo bronc.

When I worked high up in the Rocky Mountains for an outfitter for a couple of years, I found it was an excellent place to take these critters and put some distance on them. A couple of 10-day trips and they were as broke as most horses are in three months. They not only learned what long days were, they learned to navigate fast flowing rivers and narrow trails on the edges of cliffs. They could jump fallen logs and twist-'n-turn through heavy timber. They had to skid old trees to camp for firewood and carry a pack saddle, if need be. They learned what hobbles were made for and to not spook at wildlife. I still say to this day, no amount of arena riding could ever produce a better all around using horse.

But I never was much good at riding a bucking horse. Oh, I tried, all right, especially if someone was watching. Lordy, there is nothing in the world more embarrassing than kissing the ground with someone watching. With the first next two days. Then I stepped up on him. He was a sweetheart if I ever rode one. He gave willingly to the bit and was soon turning and stopping like a saint. The next day he was backing a couple of steps when asked, and keeping his head in real good position. By the third day we were loping slow circles in the pen, and I was in love with his willing disposition.

Because he was a stallion, I locked all the horses away from the centre paddock the next day, when we took our first outside ride. He acted so nice, I was kind of wishing I owned him — until I dismounted to put him back into the pen to unsaddle. I barely got the pen gate open and for no reason at all, he blew. With his first jump into the pen, he was kicking holes in the sky with those back feet. Two more wicked jumps and bang, just like that he quit. He turned around and came back to me, rubbing his head on my shoulder, all apologetic for his ungentlemanly behaviour. I tightened the cinch and worked him another 10 minutes in the pen, going over what he had already learned, to try and figure out what the problem was. He was as good as gold.

Once I had him unsaddled, I checked his back for anything sore, then checked the saddle and blanket for something that might be bugging him. I couldn't find anything, so I figured something weird was going on in his head.

I have always firmly believed that the sooner you get horses out of the corrals and put some distance on them in the open, the better they are for it. Get them out and give

them something easy to do besides going around in circles —
follow a cow or two or take them down through the timber
and get them turning through the trees. So that weekend I
spent the morning teaching him to load and unload nicely
from the trailer and then loaded him up to head about
7 miles from my home. Here was the perfect training area —
six quarters of secluded, unfenced timber with lots of trails
through it.

Due to advancing age and one too many broken bones
in the past, I did something I never used to do when young.
I took a cell phone with me and phoned a friend. I told her
where I was, what I was doing, and gave her instructions to
call an ambulance if I didn't phone her within two hours,
because I was going to need one.

The sorrel was super. We covered a lot of ground and he
worked like a pro, although he was prone to whistle a shrill
stallion call once in awhile, showing me his mind wasn't entirely on the job at hand. When a gelding from a good half mile
away answered him, he pulled a real studly act for a few minutes until I got his mind back on me. Then he was good again.

For the next three days it poured rain and I was unable
to ride him. When the sun finally surfaced, we worked in the
corral for awhile, then headed for the tall timber again. I
unloaded him and phoned my friend with the same
instructions.

I laid the cell phone on the truck seat, tightened the
stallion's cinch, led him around a bit, and then stepped up.

Lights Out!

He took a few steps, and then he blew. There was no reason for it, and no warning. He snapped me back in that saddle hard. I knew I couldn't ride him, because he had yanked all the slack out of the reins and had free access to buck uncontrolled. But I intended to give it my best shot. I had never before gone for the saddle horn on a bucking horse, but I did this time. I got a death grip on that baby and hollered at him to give it his best shot. He was hitting the ground so hard he was grunting with every jump. For a spilt second, I fancied that I was good enough to stay with him. Then I lost my grip on the saddle horn!

If you lose your grip when you're leaning back to ride those hard hitting jumps, then you're going off over the back end. I remember everything as clear as if it were yesterday. As if in slow motion, I passed over his rump, just as he was kicking high. I felt him connecting with me again while I was in midair. Then the ground came up to meet me, and it was lights out!

I know I was unconscious for about 20 minutes, because I remember looking at my watch just before I stepped up on him. I looked again when I came to. I remembered that I was to phone my friend to let her know I was okay when I got back to the parked truck and trailer. There was the truck only a few yards from me. But why was I lying on the ground? I rolled over and there was a horse, calmly grazing. Whose horse was that? And where was its owner? He must be pretty stupid to let his horse graze with the reins dragging on the ground.

I got to my feet and except for feeling kind of numb in my head and neck, I seemed okay. I figured I better catch that horse before he stepped on his reins and hurt his mouth. The horse stood quietly for me to catch it. Now what was I going to do with it? I looked around. Where was its owner? I didn't have all day to stand there holding onto a horse.

I was feeling kind of dizzy, so I decided to load the horse into my trailer until the owner showed up.

The stallion stepped up in the trailer nice and proper, just like a horse I would have taught how to load. I closed the end gate and moved weakly around to the driver's side of the truck. There lay a horse halter and lead rope. My halter and lead rope. Everything came rushing back then. I sat down hard, as my confused mind adjusted.

I decided I had better not drive. I would phone my friend and tell her to come get me, but I couldn't remember her number. I couldn't remember any of my friends' numbers. I phoned the operator, but didn't get very far because I couldn't remember their last names either. Because I didn't want to just sit there waiting for someone to happen along and help me, I figured I'd slowly make my way home. I knew it wasn't far. I turned the truck around and drove to the highway, but didn't know which way to turn. I chose left, and thankfully it was the correct choice.

It was over a week before my scrambled brains began to function normally. I'd wake up in the morning, pick up my brassiere and wonder what to do with it. I'd put it down and get dressed but forget my socks because they were out of sight in a drawer. I'd try to brush my hair with my toothbrush and curse it for being such a pathetic hairbrush. And my teeth, well they just didn't get brushed. If they did, I don't want to remember what I brushed them with!

For the most part, the good old days are gone. People breed horses these days for specific traits and good dispositions. Some breed for the characteristics of English horses — tall horses of great strength and beauty. Some breed horses specifically for working cattle in arenas — little fellows that are catty and quick, with the desire to get down and look a cow in the eye. Some breed strictly for racing — horses with unbelievable speed on a straightaway. Some for perfect conformation — horses meant to take your breath away with their regal bearing. For every discipline out there asked of a horse, someone, somewhere breeds specifically for that.

A growing number of horses are handled from birth by owners with sympathetic understanding of their physical and mental needs. It's been years since I ran across a horse who didn't know what grain in a bucket was or had never felt a rope around his neck before taking his first walk into the centre of a colt starting pen.

And that is the way it should be as we move into the future. But you know, I still miss the old days. Sometimes I even dream about them, when I'm lying in bed, with the lights out.

About the Author

Gayle Bunney grew up in Alberta, where she rode horses over Canada's vast expanse of prairie. It's a place where you can ride from sunup to sundown while you share your day with the horse beneath you, the prairie wildlife, and the contented herds of cattle grazing the land. She also spent many years riding mountain trails where she discovered a whole new offering of Mother Nature's supreme beauty. And the horse was always a part of her very existence.

From stallions to newborn foals, people-loving horses to man-hating beasts, creatures of beauty to the homely old faithful, all have found a place in her heart. Her years spent breeding, training, doctoring, and learning the subtle language spoken by the horse is her life's work.

Now residing in Bonnyville, Alberta, Gayle is content raising small breed ankle biters and top of the line quarter horses. She is the author of two other books: *Horse Stories*, *Riding the Wind* and *My Life with Dogs*.

RIDING ON THE WILD SIDE
Tales of Adventure in the Canadian West

"Suddenly, there was a crashing noise to our left and out of the timber came about 20 head of horses and a few bewildered elk followed by a couple of yelling cowboys."

This fascinating collection of stories is about working horses and the people who make a living riding them in Canada's mountain national parks. Imagine chasing a herd of wild horses, galloping at full speed toward an impenetrable forest ... and you get a sense of the excitement of the backcountry life.

 True stories. Truly Canadian.

ISBN 1-55153-985-3

LEGENDARY SHOW JUMPERS
The Incredible Stories of Great Canadian Horses

"He could be so gentle and quiet, but when he got in the ring he got so excited we couldn't hold him. ...But I wasn't afraid of him."
Louis Welsh on Barra Lad

Once in a while a horse comes along that is extraordinary. Air Pilot, Barra Lad, and Big Ben have all had their turn at being the brightest star blazing in the show-jumping sky. For more than 100 years, great Canadian high-flying horses have provided spectators with exhilarating displays of their jaw-dropping talent and love of jumping.

 True stories. Truly Canadian.

ISBN 1-55153-980-2

AMAZING STORIES™

STOLEN HORSES

Intriguing Tales of Rustling and Rescues

ANIMAL/CRIME
by Dorothy Pedersen

STOLEN HORSES
Intriguing Tales of Rustling and Rescues

"Horse theft is on the rise...and can be traced throughout history... I found it very interesting to read about the people affected by these crimes."
Frankie Chesler, Canadian Equestrian
Team Rider/Show Jumping

Dorothy Pedersen dishes up the dirt on equine crime in Canada. The horse rustling business is alive and thriving, but the valiant efforts of those who track down stolen horses are an inspiration. In this collection of true stories, the author delivers an intriguing look into this nefarious aspect of the horse world.

 True stories. Truly Canadian.

ISBN 1-55153-971-3

GREAT DOG STORIES
Inspirational Tales About
Exceptional Dogs

"His name is not wild dog anymore, but the first friend, because he will be our friend for always and always and always."
Rudyard Kipling

Dogs have long acted as protectors, but they are also an inspiration to many people who work closely with them. From seeing-eye dogs to tracking dogs, the bond formed with canine companions can be exceptionally rewarding. The author features the stories of nine incredible dogs and their owners.

 True stories. Truly Canadian.

ISBN 1-55153-946-2

OTHER AMAZING STORIES

These titles are available wherever you buy books. If you have trouble finding the book you want, call the Altitude order desk at **1-800-957-6888**, e-mail your request to: **orderdesk@altitudepublishing.com** or visit our Web site at **www.amazingstories.ca**

New AMAZING STORIES titles are published every month.